On Argentina and
the Southern Cone

Globalizing Regions

Globalizing Regions offers concise accounts of how the nations and regions of the world are experiencing the effects of globalization. Richly descriptive yet theoretically informed, each volume shows how individual places are navigating the tension between age-old traditions and the new forces generated by globalization.

On Argentina and the Southern Cone

Neoliberalism and National Imaginations

ALEJANDRO GRIMSON

AND

GABRIEL KESSLER

Routledge
Taylor & Francis Group
New York London

Published in 2005 by
Routledge
Taylor & Francis Group
270 Madison Avenue
New York, NY 10016

Published in Great Britain by
Routledge
Taylor & Francis Group
2 Park Square
Milton Park, Abingdon
Oxon OX14 4RN

© 2005 by Taylor & Francis Group, LLC
Routledge is an imprint of Taylor & Francis Group

Printed in the United States of America on acid-free paper
10 9 8 7 6 5 4 3 2 1

International Standard Book Number-10: 0-415-94763-4 (Hardcover) 0-415-94764-2 (Softcover)
International Standard Book Number-13: 978-0-415-94763-3 (Hardcover) 978-0-415-94764-0 (Softcover)
Library of Congress Card Number 2005008894

Library of Congress Cataloging-in-Publication Data

Grimson, Alejandro.
    On Argentina and the Southern Cone : neoliberalism and national imaginations / Alejandro Grimson and Gabriel Kessler ; translated by Margaret Westwell.
        p. cm. -- (Globalizing regions)
    Includes bibliographical references and index.
    ISBN 0-415-94763-4 (hb : alk. paper) -- ISBN 0-415-94764-2 (pb : alk. paper)
    1. Argentina--History--1983-2002. 2. Argentina--History--2002- 3. MERCOSUR (Organization) 4. Globalization--Political aspects--Argentina. 5. Globalization--Social aspects--Argentina. 6. Emigration and immigration--Social aspects. 7. Marginality, Social--Argentina--History. I. Kessler, Gabriel, 1964- II. Title. III. Series: Globalizing regions series.

F2849 .2.G75 2005
982--dc22   2005008894

Taylor & Francis Group
is the Academic Division of T&F Informa plc.

Visit the Taylor & Francis Web site at
http://www.taylorandfrancis.com

and the Routledge Web site at
http://www.routledge-ny.com

Introduction

States and nations are redefining their place in the world at the present time in the wake of the economic, political, and cultural transnationalization processes that have occurred in recent decades. Each country, each city, each region is seeking to recast its role and potential in accord with its geographical location, its history, and the times. This positioning is, of course, conditioned by multiple factors, which include conditions of production, economic and geopolitical interests, and sociocultural characteristics as well.

Within this global situation Argentina in particular, and the Southern Cone in general, are particularly interesting cases. The historical profile of Argentina and of the way Argentines imagine their place in the world have been greatly changed by neoliberalism and the current phase of globalization.

Argentina is a country that has been marked by extreme situations. Like the United States, Canada, and Australia at the end of the nineteenth and the beginning of the twentieth centuries, it received wave after wave of European immigrants. At the end of the twentieth century, it had one of the highest per capita foreign debts in the world. Of the Latin American countries subjected to a military dictatorship during the 1970s, Argentina had the most "disappeared" people, around ten times more than Chile and one hundred times more than Brazil. During the 1980s it was one of the few countries to suffer chronic hyperinflation. On the positive side of the ledger, Argentina has one of the highest levels of education in Latin America and a large middle class.

Frequently studying extreme cases helps shed light on general questions of social life. The Argentine case is very useful for questioning certain theoretical, political, and journalistic commonplaces regarding globalization and neoliberalism. This book analyzes both how Argentina sought to insert itself in regional and global processes and how global ideas and policies were appropriated and applied in Argentina in particular, and in the Southern Cone in general. This may help clarify why classic neoliberalism can and should be considered a thing of the past.

Writing a book in English on Argentina for readers unfamiliar with the country presents several dilemmas. For example, how to transmit an adequate image of a country that is as far below the economic and social standards of developed countries as it is above those of the planet's poorest countries. A national narrative imposed a destiny on a country and, in the case of Argentines, once again we find extremes: intrepid optimists have no doubt that, notwithstanding events of recent years, if Argentina follows certain prescriptions, its level of development will immediately rise, whereas the pessimists are sure that, unless it drastically changes course right away, it will present one of the most devastating scenes in the world a few years hence.

In our view a careful examination of the present situation is preferable to any attempt at foretelling the future. In 2002 more than 40 percent of the Argentine population was living in poverty, more than in Brazil or Mexico, twice as many as in

Chile, and very close to poverty figures in Bolivia, El Salvador, and Paraguay. Unemployment was around 15 percent, double that in Brazil, and six times higher than the rate in Mexico (Cepal 2003). Nevertheless these figures hide a complex, heterogeneous country. In Buenos Aires middle-class neighborhoods that bring to mind Europe for foreign tourists coexist with severe malnutrition.

The Argentine crisis, images of which went around the world in 2001 and 2002, marked the collapse of an economic and social model and also the eclipse of a set of social images and narratives regarding the place of Argentina in the world. As a result, not only is a particular economic policy being questioned but also serious damage has been done to a cultural mind-set, the extent of which it is still too early to evaluate. In other words the way Argentina fit itself into the increasingly globalized world that opened up in the late 1980s, as well as the specific way Washington Consensus policies were adopted, was a result neither of contingencies nor of the particular personality of the Argentine president. On the contrary, the social, political, and economic history of this period grew, in large part, out of the traditional way Argentines imagined themselves and their country in the world.

Argentina had convinced itself and at least a part of the rest of the world that it was a European enclave in Latin America. People proudly affirmed, in accordance with the racist ideology of the era, that Argentina was a country with no African-born or indigenous population. Two trivial but significant examples illustrate the point. In 1921, when the Brazilian soccer team was preparing to play in Buenos Aires, the Brazilian president asked that no mulattos (and certainly no blacks) be included on the team in order to improve the country's image in Argentina; the last time the Brazilian team had played there, the Argentine press referred to the visiting players as "little Macaque monkeys." Anthropology, the discipline created in the West to study "others"—those who are different (non-Westerners)—sent some of its leading lights to Brazil, Peru, Bolivia, and Mexico, among other countries. But no anthropologist of the stature of Lévi-Strauss, Redfield, or Balandier ever researched in Argentina.

The above is more the consequence of the commonly held image of the country than a reflection of its sociodemographic profile. Actually, Argentina has more indigenous people relative to its population than Brazil, and in absolute terms the number is about the same. In addition a large part of the population shares European and indigenous ancestry.

In sum the sociodemographic profile, degree of civil rights, political characteristics, and social imagery of any given nation are intertwined. A brief review of the interrelated factors that got the country into this situation in the first place is required to get to the bottom of how neoliberalism and globalization transformed Argentina from the 1980s on.

HOW THE STATE AND THE NATION WERE FORMED

Looking at a map of South America, one naturally questions why there are so many different countries. If the area was principally dominated by two colonial powers, the Spanish and the Portuguese, how did ten different nation-states come into being? In fact, contemporary frontiers are the result of a whole group of factors, among which colonial confrontations are but a single chapter. Others include the individual political and commercial interests of the administrative jurisdictions of the three Spanish Viceroyalties in South America (one in

Peru, one in Río de la Plata, and one in New Granada); the wars among the fledgling countries following independence, such as the one between Buenos Aires and Río de Janeiro in the 1820s that led to the creation of Uruguay as buffer state between the two; and the neocolonial interventions on the part of the United States fewer than one hundred years ago, such as the one that split Panama from Colombia.

None of the present-day frontiers in South America correspond to geographical divisions of indigenous societies that predated the arrival of Spaniards and Portuguese. This is pertinent in the case of Argentina, because in their search for historical antecedents for the founding of the Argentine nation, nationalist historians had no point of reference corresponding to the Inca, Aztec, or Mayan civilizations in other countries. In a word, the existence of Argentina obviously owes nothing to "race," "ethnic group," or any feeling of belonging predating independence. Indeed, in 1810, the year Argentina became independent from Spain, not even its name—Argentina—had national significance.

Why, then, does Argentina exist? The overriding reasons are clearly economic and political, not cultural. In 1778 the King of Spain created the Viceroyalty of the Río de la Plata, whose seat was Buenos Aires, because, as silver mining in Potosí, Bolivia, began to decline, the beef and hides so easily come by on the Pampa grasslands became increasingly attractive.

In 1810, when the independence process began, the word *Argentina* referred not to the nation but rather to someone from Buenos Aires or the Río de la Plata region. The advance of the term *Argentina* after Independence constituted an early expression of the hegemony of Buenos Aires over other provincial cities. Linguistic domination is "a precedent for the early centralist tendencies" for making "the new nation dependent on this city: tendencies resisted by the majority of Río de la Plata cities" (Chiaramonte 1997, 70).

After the Independence wars, which ended in 1826, Buenos Aires maintained its monopoly over foreign trade and custom duties collected. But this supremacy of the port city over provincial capitals does not suffice to explain the predominance of the image of Buenos Aires as a European enclave. For this, an examination of how the Argentine state evolved is necessary: the state as instrument for constructing increasingly important institutions from public schools to the Armed Forces; as instrument for broadening—not necessarily lineally—the scope of civil rights at certain key times during the twentieth century; and as an instrument for constructing, by means of these same institutions and civil rights, along with other symbolic mechanisms, the narratives that will give meaning to the term *Argentina*. To lay the foundation for understanding globalization and neoliberal reform in Argentina, we briefly consider five key dates: 1880, 1930, 1945, 1976, and 1999.

1880: A NATION FOR A DESERT

The modern Argentine state came into being in 1880 because, although the National Constitution was signed in 1853, the conflict between the port of Buenos Aires and the provinces was not decided until then. The War of the Triple Alliance, in which Argentina joined with Brazil and Uruguay to economically and socially decimate Paraguay, was a key factor in the construction of the institution of a national army. This war also played a major role in Brazil becoming a nation-state. According to certain Brazilian authors, it marked the beginning of real national feeling (Carvalho 1990, 32). For its part, Argentina's entry into the war was initially viewed through the lens of the civil wars between the port city and the provinces, and this awakened resistance. But as it was a response to a foreign invasion—Paraguayans had crossed over into Argentina—"Argentine participation acquired a national dimension" (Halperín Donghi 1995, 56). In the course of the war, local militias and provincial armies became subordinated to the central power. And afterward, internecine struggles subsided as the state set out to destroy indigenous populations to establish control over its territory, especially Patagonia.

This was part of the strategy for what Halperín Donghi called "a nation for the Argentine desert." Laws promoting immigration, public education, and the creation of diverse national institutions had paved the way for nation-building prior to 1880. The agro-export economic model, which lasted until 1930, was initiated at this time. It was an era dominated by a "liberal" elite and characterized by strong state intervention. If Argentina consumed 50 percent of all the newsprint consumed in Latin America in 1930, it marked the success of the program to create a nationwide public school system. If the country could boast of a semiskilled workforce, efforts on the part of the state to attract foreign investment could take the credit, the same state that was making government land available for raising wheat and cattle.

The modern Argentine state came into being by articulating a particular model of capital accumulation and a certain social image regarding Argentina's place in the world that has lasted until the present time: Argentina as "breadbasket of the world." But, as is the case for the key dates to follow, different migratory processes must also be taken into account when constructing a generally accepted national narrative. During this first period, it was the shiploads of Europeans disembarking in Buenos Aires.

The process was certainly not smooth: union and political leaders and anarchists from abroad were persecuted, their presence as foreigners on Argentine soil being contrasted unfavorably to the nationalistic depiction of *criollos* and *gauchos*. This occurred in a context in which 70 percent of the workforce in Buenos Aires was foreign born. But during this period, and especially after mass migration from abroad had ceased, history books viewed the European immigrant as indispensable for progress and modernization (see Rofman and Romero 1973). Indeed, immigration had the dual objective of rapidly increasing the population and, above all, "consolidating Europe's civilizing influence" (Halperín Donghi 1987, 201).

Many xenophobic characteristics were reworked when incorporated into the definitive narrative of the birth of the Argentine nation: the immigrants became an integral part of the modern nation-state; the need for a workforce became translated into the slogans "settle the desert" and "to govern is to settle"[1] (expressed in the 1853 Constitution, which guaranteed basic rights to "all men—and not just citizens—in the world who want to live on Argentine soil"). This led to one of the largest mass migrations in modern history, in proportional terms.

Argentina was a country that, in comparison to its native population, received one of the largest contingents of European immigrants ever recorded. It is also the country that, of the immigrants who came, retained the least number: between 1870 and 1929, the percentage of immigrants staying on was 54 percent, a considerably lower percentage than the 66 percent retained by the United States during the same period (Torrado 2003, 94).

This is the framework within which the modern state developed its nation-building strategy of "Argentinization."

Along with public education, the army (which employed universal conscription) became one of the key bulwarks against cosmopolitan tendencies (see Rouquié 1981). This Argentinization of European immigrants became part of the progress promised by the nation. In spite of its conflicts and contradictions, then, the immigrant process was an integral part of the story of how the Argentine nation was born.

The public school is a condensed version of the national equation according to which cultural homogenization carries with it the implicit promise of social mobility. Spreading quickly, public education became a source of new historical narratives whose protagonists were national heroes; it was also a source of citizenship and a mechanism for social mobility. That these narratives were credible and became fixed in the public mind is owing to the existence of other rights and opportunities that were becoming increasingly available. And this positive image of public education has lasted: even in the worst moments of the crises to come, the student population continued to grow, the poorest sectors of the population entering the educational system and doing everything possible to stay there. As a result of the significance education has in Argentina, research shows that, unlike the case in other Latin American countries, even among the most marginalized sectors of society in the 1990s, education was seen as the most important path to social mobility and respect; in other words, in spite of being in crisis, faith in public schools has been maintained.

1930: THE FIRST MILITARY COUP

When Wall Street crashed in 1929, one side effect was a balance of payments crisis in Argentina. When prices for wheat and beef fell on the world market and exports plummeted, foreign investors withdrew capital from Argentina and returned home. The severe crisis in the agro-export sector dragged down other social sectors, setting off growing unemployment and infla- tion, which, in turn, eroded popular support for the constitu- tional government.

Following the political and economic crisis in 1930, Argentina began using a new accumulation model for indus- trializing based on "import substitution," or a method of fostering and protecting domestic industries that enjoy pre- ferred treatment vis-à-vis foreign firms. Industrial growth between 1935 and 1937 almost equaled growth between 1914 and 1935. Although the economic model was different, the importance of a workforce remained key. Both the number of workplaces and of workers doubled in ten years' time.

This implied an increase in the demand for labor, which meant that import substitution coexisted with urbanization: 1930 marked the beginning of a period of mass migration, from the provinces to the city of Buenos Aires. This internal migration transformed daily life in Buenos Aires and made its white middle- class residents feel that their world had been "invaded" by these provincial "foreigners" they referred to as *cabecitas negras,* or "little black heads." And here yet another Argentine contradiction arises: in a country with few Afro-descendants and supposedly "without blacks," *los negros*—the racist connotation of *cabecita negra* is evident—are the majority population.

The idea of Argentina as a European enclave in South America goes back to the second half of the nineteenth cen- tury, but it gained renewed impetus after 1930 when mass European immigration ended. Argentina's neighbors were strongly influenced by this view. According to them, Argentina was not a part of Latin America, which was represented by the indigenous majority in Bolivia or Paraguay or by the Afro-descendants in Brazil.

This image of Argentina as a country with a homogeneous population of Euro-descendants is not so much false as incomplete: it becomes credible when Buenos Aires is thought of as synonymous with Argentina, relegating the rest of the population to the category of second-class citizens and foreigners in their own country. And thus it was that when the descendants of native people and of native people and Spaniards made their way en masse to Buenos Aires to work in factories, they were viewed as foreign and referred to as *cabecitas negras*.

Historically divided politically and territorially into capital city and provinces, Argentina had excluded *negros* from the image of the prototypical Argentine, who was said to have descended from the ship passengers who arrived from Europe. Hence Argentina was ripe for conflict when the *cabecitas negras* emigrated en masse from the provinces to the port city of Buenos Aires. The result was the birth of Peronism as a new national narrative in which the protagonist was this new social actor, the provincial immigrant. The story went on to depict a national strategy for politically integrating the popular masses into the mainstream as "the backbone" of the governing party. For this to happen, it was necessary to reformulate the role of the state to integrate this formerly marginalized part of the population into society politics.

In spite of the resulting conflicts, the immigrants arriving from Europe during the first mass migratory process were integrated by a national strategy according to which the Argentine state granted legitimacy in exchange for ideological and cultural homogenization. Ultimately, Peronism incorporated the provincial immigrants as members of an industrial working class.

A historical narrative that lasted decades began in 1945: the national-popular state. Its first chapter was the indissoluble pact between Juan Domingo Perón and the people who had arisen out of the events of October 17, 1945. On that day provincial immigrant factory hands made their political debut by marching to the *Plaza de Mayo* and demanding the liberation of their leader, who had been jailed by the same military men who had taken power with him in a coup two years before. An alliance that identified the leader with the people was forged. It outlived political banishment and exile, and was capitalized on, after the leader's death, by various self-proclaimed successors. The pact also marked the beginning of the irreconcilable dichotomy of Peronists–anti-Peronists, a division that aligned factions as varied as liberals, leftists, and Catholics, among others, before it was erased.

Peronism has been a political phenomenon difficult to typify for Argentines and foreigners alike. Although defying traditional categories, Peronism undoubtedly constitutes what political scientists term a national-popular model. But much more than a form of government, Peronism became the narrative dominating Argentine political life for decades afterwards, not only because of its duration but also because it articulated subnarratives for all levels of social life, including the family, the state, unions, youth, women, and so on. Its story line was also complex enough to include an institutional prototype and economic strategy, as well as its own symbolism and aesthetic values. According to Martuccelli and Svampa (1997), Peronist economic policy was based on import substitution and the development of Argentine industries, in particular mass consumption products. The success of this economic strategy depended on the increase in mass purchasing power. This led to state intervention to ensure that workers' wages increased to stimulate industrial expansion. As a result, a virtual alliance was forged between popular sectors and an industrial petit bourgeoisie protected by the state.

On the social plane Peronism implied the construction of a type of welfare state similar to the "conservative-corporative" model described by Esping-Anderson (1990). A bipolar state grants indirect social benefits to strong unions, one per sector, in exchange for political support. For non-wage earners, there was a social welfare network that included public hospitals and the Eva Perón Foundation. When put into practice, this implied recognizing rights for a large part of the newly arrived immigrants from the provinces who had been joining the labor force in the port city for several decades. It also involved subordinating any diversity associated with different migrant processes to the uniform set of categories provided by the workplace. The top-down state structure implied the creation of strong unions led by powerful union leaders. All social organizations were subsumed under Peronism, whereas traditional left-wing and anarchist labor organizations were weakened, either by co-optation or by repression.

And finally, the national-popular narrative used a new political language capable of giving public expression to the private experience of popular sectors, what Daniel James (1990), following Raymond Williams (1980), termed the "structure of feeling": the language used, the way the leader addressed his "shirtless ones," the references to the people, some of the ways in which the formerly invisible masses became incorporated into Argentine public and political life. As L.A. Romero (1994) put it, the crux of the problem posed by Peronism was

13 **Introduction**

that it was a cultural conflict. In the final analysis, even though Peronism lashed out against a vaguely defined "oligarchy" that was bent on destroying the happiness of the people, it left the economic roots of this same oligarchy intact. But Peronism was perceived by the social elite as an affront in the area of symbolic space and cultural signs. Migrants from the provinces had already been incorporated into urban life; what was new was their appearance in public in areas formerly off limits to them. Above and beyond its political significance, October 17 was symbolic for precisely that: formerly invisible masses of people from unheard-of suburbs marched downtown to the *Plaza de Mayo*, the center of economic, political, and ecclesiastic power, where in prior decades appearing without a tie would have merited arrest. This was the birth of a movement in which, in the words of L.A. Romero, "stimulated and protected by the Peronist state, and taking advantage of economic good times, popular sectors became incorporated as consumers into urban and political life" (p. 159).

A military coup in 1955 put an end to the Peronist government, but not to the omnipresence of Perón in exile. The years leading up to 1976 were defined by the ban on Peronism, a stormy political climate, and a high degree of institutional instability: several military coups and three civilian governments, not one of which fulfilled its term of office. During this time the country entered the second stage of import substitution, which was characterized by the production of capital equipment and durable consumer goods, the installation of foreign enterprises in Argentina, oil exploration, and a new relationship with the United States. Mass consumption was no longer the driving force moving the economy, and wages fell. Unions responded with a strong campaign in defense of their members' earning power, this being the extraparliamentary expression of the banned Peronist party. A large part of the cosmopolitan, urban middle class began a process of economic and cultural modernization that revolutionized their consumption patterns and way of life. Psychoanalysis appeared on the scene, along with aesthetic vanguards, intensifying the division between an authoritarian, unstable institutional life and an active sociocultural life exercised with a certain margin of autonomy.

Between 1955 and 1976, within the dichotomy of Peronists–anti-Peronists and the confrontations between the left and right wings of Peronism itself, Argentine society played out its alternatives. Alliances were tenuous, but the dichotomy, and the mutual belief that the triumph of the adversary would bring about disaster and ruin the country, made the 1960s a highly turbulent decade. In 1968 the worker-student demonstration and confrontation called the *Cordobazo* took place; Peronist (mainly the Montoneros) and left-wing groups—the most important of which was the Ejército Revolucionario del Pueblo (ERP)—became increasingly radicalized, and paramilitary forces—the Argentine Anti-Communist Alliance—formed and began killing political militants and intellectuals. The political situation became polarized to the breaking point. In 1973 a sick Perón returned to Argentina, where he died in office one year later. He was succeeded by his wife and vice president, Isabel Martínez de Perón, whose ineptitude accentuated the tension between Peronist factions. Economic chaos spread, and the inevitable military coup in 1976 was received with indifference, if not approval, by a large part of the Argentine population.

1976: STATE TERRORISM AND ECONOMIC DESTRUCTURING

The coup in 1976 marked the beginning of the darkest period in Argentine history, a time characterized by a systematic campaign of terror carried out by the state and leading to the disappearance, torture, and murder of 30,000 men and women. The military saw their mission as "saving the country" by disciplining a society incapable of disciplining itself. They decided to do away with anyone and anything that stood in its way to make a clean slate of the past and begin all over again. The image of a society in need of discipline because of a lack of self-regulatory power reappears in Argentine history in times of crisis, and this was no exception. The same metaphor was resurrected in the 1990s with a democratic government in power. In this latter case, fiscal discipline was the regulating medium that saved a society whose social bonds were frayed to the breaking point during the 1989–1990 hyperinflation.

Telling the story of dictatorship is a problem in Argentina. By emphasizing sinister repressive and economic policies exclusively, there is a risk of failing to account for the structural processes that allowed the dictatorship to take power in the first place. But when the emphasis is placed on the set of conditions that brought about the 1976 coup, including the social consensus it enjoyed and the authoritarian elements characterizing so many political forces, there is a risk of losing sight of the different methods available of wielding power and the individual responsibility of specific actors.

Be that as it may, it was during the dictatorship that began in 1976 that economic power moved from the agro-export and industrial sectors to the financial sector of the economy. In a highly speculative financial context, where profit margins for financial operations were far superior to those for industrial production, what came to be termed the "sweet money" era was born. The repeal of all trade barriers occurred at the same time, dealing the deathblow to Argentine industry and the industrial workforce and greatly reducing the average wage. Foreign debt, impoverishment, and the destructuring of the productive system are the three keys to the first neoliberal chapter in Argentina, issues that reappeared in altered form during the 1990s.

And when the economic crisis threatened to get out of hand during the dictatorship, General Galtieri laid hands on one of the few symbols capable of uniting Argentines: he invaded the Falkland Islands. Political organizations almost across the board responded by supporting this unquestionably nationalistic crusade. In the beginning the government was successful: the call to revindicate an old demand for sovereignty drew broad social support. However, the rapid defeat of the Argentine Armed Forces by Great Britain accelerated the fall of the dictatorship, and the democratically elected government of Raúl Alfonsín took office in 1983.

State terrorism constitutes a major turning point in Argentine history. The marks and memories it left have transformed every aspect of social life, whose definitive form is still not clear. The feeling shared by Argentines in general when it ended was "Never Again," the title of the report delivered by the commission that investigated the brutal acts perpetuated during those years. Since that time, in spite of the severe crises that have swept Argentina, democracy was never under threat nor did any sign of the desire to invoke an authoritarian form of government over a society incapable of governing itself appear as had happened so often in the past.

Another key moment came during the presidency of Raúl Alfonsín: the hyperinflation of 1989. As we show in the following pages, the everyday instability, the impossibility of making plans, and the breaking of social bonds and contracts brought about by persistent hyperinflation (during which time prices increased several times a day) left lasting social fears and marked two key foundations: the evisceration of political life carried out by the dictatorship and the bludgeoning of social life by the hyperinflation of the late 1980s. Ironically, Carlos Saúl Menem, a Peronist leader from a poor northern province, put into practice the neoliberal policies that liquidated the national-popular model that the same political force had built.

To understand the 1990s, one must understand the alliance between Perón—as well as his heirs—and the people. Only Menem's Peronist government could put an end to the existing cleavage and establish a formerly unthinkable alliance between Peronism and liberal sectors closely related in Argentine social imagery to the hated oligarchy of the old days. The neoliberal narrative dissolved old political antagonisms by claiming that the common good consisted of economic stability and a market economy, which is not debatable politically, and whose legitimacy no "social cost" puts in doubt. And with regard to alliances, anything goes. What Peronism gave birth to—the national-popular state—was dismantled by a Peronist government decades later. Is this an irony of history? Is it an act of treason against basic principles? It was said in Argentina during the 1990s—and it is hard to deny—that only a Peronist government could have undertaken a reform that would have such a devastating effect on popular sectors, the bedrock of its political support. This social consensus was, and still is (as we show in the pages that follow), a question that is as controversial as it is critical.

And so it was that the 1990s were marked by a neo-liberal hegemony and the systematic application of its policies.

Although in general terms—as was the case with the 1976 dictatorship—all Southern Cone countries followed Argentina's lead, it should also be noted that the differences were not insignificant. Some countries, such as Uruguay, applied the neoliberal prescription much more moderately than Argentina. Others, Chile for example, are still considered examples of the model's success. But although data show a reduction in poverty, they do not show that inequality levels were as high as ever.

THE BOOK

Generally, we examine sociocultural transformations taking place in Argentina during the 1990s and up to the present time, as well as the regional repercussions of these transformations. After depicting the different ways territory, state, and society have been conceptualized over the course of Argentine history, we analyze in the first chapter the relations between Argentina and its neighbors in recent years, as well as the Mercosur project and changes occurring along the borders in member countries. Specifically, we examine the way in which certain characteristics of the welfare state interacted with a long-standing strategic scenario positing war between Argentina and Brazil or Chile in the mid-twentieth century and then contrast that with regional integration under the neoliberal era that followed.

In the second chapter we analyze the structural changes taking place during the 1990s—both the transformations in state and economy and the construction of a narrative legitimizing neoliberalism. We contrast these changes with what took place in Uruguay and Chile during the same period of time.

In the third chapter we cover the social impact of the reforms analyzed in the preceding chapter. Concretely, we focus on five social sectors: the traditionally poor, the impoverished middle class, the unemployed, the winners, and young people who combine work with petty crime to survive. At the end of the chapter we make a comparison with events in Uruguay and Chile, which sheds further light on the case of Argentina.

In the fourth chapter we cover the changing role of ethnicity in Argentina. We examine alterations brought about by neoliberal policies in the workplace in the context of a development project and link that to the meaning ascribed by Argentines to immigrants from border and nonborder countries. In addition, we update the view of Argentina as a European enclave with first world status in a continent populated by native people, mestizos, and Afro-descendants. We then contrast that with the contemporary diversity politics developed by subordinate groups on one hand and international agencies on the other.

In the fifth chapter we describe the social and collective responses to the new economic, scale, and political situation arising during the 1990s: the barter phenomenon, road blocking by *piqueteros,* common meal centers, and failed businesses, seized and reopened by workers, among other responses. In the course of this chapter it becomes clear that the belief that neoliberal reform was passively accepted in Argentina is as shortsighted as the view of a "red Argentina" where the neoliberal consensus turned into a massive struggle against globalization in the blink of an eye.

We close with a discussion of the theoretical and political relevance of the Argentine case for analyzing the consequences of neoliberalism, and of the globalization process.

Territory, Nation and Mercosur
One

Reforms in the 1990s transformed the ways in which both nation and state had been structured up to that time. New concepts began circulating about Argentina's place in the region and the world on the two dimensions of any nation-state project—people and sovereignty. Ideas and policies on citizenship changed, and new ways of conceiving national territory and frontiers emerged.

In this chapter we examine the changes occurring in relations between Argentina and neighboring countries, within the general framework of ongoing regionalization processes. Specifically, we analyze Mercosur—the regional trading bloc that emerged in the 1990s—and its discontents from the perspective of the broad repercussions on social and cultural processes that followed the signing of the Treaty for Regional Integration. The mere existence of this trading bloc signaled a sea change in regional geopolitical relations: in an increasingly globalized world, the old policies of confrontation between Argentina and Chile on one hand and Brazil on the other no longer made sense—if they ever had.

Current regionalization and globalization processes have not erased frontiers between countries but instead altered the way they function and the meaning ascribed to them. In a word, the frequently heard announcement of "the end of frontiers" has no juridical, institutional, or sociocultural basis. Contrary to opinion in some quarters, "deterritorialization" has not occurred; one territorialization process has been exchanged for another. Concretely, frontiers have not been erased in the Southern Cone; their function and meaning have changed, but in many ways they are stronger than ever.

Contrasting present-day frontiers with mid-twentieth-century ones clearly points up the differences between two territorialization models, the latter characterizing the import-substitution economic model and the former, neoliberalism. In the course of this model change, Argentina has acquired a new regional role, particularly with regard to Brazil. Fifty years ago Argentina was considered "more developed" than Brazil. But since the beginning of the present century, Argentina has been the prototypical country in crisis, whereas her neighbor to the north has progressed significantly.

Our point of departure for studying these processes is how national identity images were constructed in the first place, and how they are being recycled at the present time. Stigmas and prejudices persist on both sides of the border, so any analysis of the sociocultural dimensions of Mercosur "integration projects" must take them into account. Assuming that macroeconomic "integration processes" have direct, immediate effects on the cultures involved is to lose sight of the preexisting historical and political dimension, as well as of the differentiated social interests and strong feelings of belonging of the people living along any given border.

TWO FOUNDING PROCESSES

The founding of Argentina was the result of internal and external pressure. During the nineteenth century foreign pressure was applied by Britain and Spain in particular. Despite the failure of the English invasions (1806 and 1807) and the ultimate success of the wars of independence (1816), strong commercial and diplomatic ties were maintained with Britain until midway through the twentieth century.

The key period in territorial terms within the country was the so-called Conquest of the Desert. The Indians had been losing ground ever since the Spaniards arrived. But it wasn't until the late nineteenth century that the Argentine state mounted a systematic military campaign to establish its hegemony once and for all. Following the massacre of the native people in Patagonia, the modern Argentine state was founded.

The success of this campaign ensured the hegemony of Buenos Aires and its port over the interests of the provinces. Thus, the agro-export economic model was born, and along with it the fantasy that Argentina was the granary of the world. Another important institution was customs; the duty it collected on imports and exports provided the tax revenues necessary for running the nation.

Organizing the country around the port of Buenos Aires implied that all trains and trucks converged there to unload raw materials from all over the country for export and to pick up imported manufactured goods. Interestingly enough, in the early twentieth century to get from Salta in the north of the country to Mendoza in the center, one had to pass through Buenos Aires. And one still does to this day, because airlines and many long distance bus companies have their hub in the port city. It is also administrative and politically impossible to bypass the city of Buenos Aires, a situation nicely synthesized by provincial inhabitants when they say, "God is everywhere, but his headquarters are in Buenos Aires."

In terms of urban primacy—the population of a country's largest city in relation to that of other important cities—Buenos Aires is a continental leader: in 2001, 45.5 percent of the urban population of Argentina lived in metropolitan Buenos Aires; in Brazil the corresponding figure for metropolitan Río de Janeiro and Sao Paulo was 22.5 percent in 2000; and in Mexico only 27.4 percent of the urban population lived in Mexico City in 2002.

The political and cultural preponderance of the city of Buenos Aires over the rest of the country is equally overwhelming. In point of fact, not only do Buenos Aires residents attribute national significance to what happens in their native city but also even researchers extrapolate to the country at large empirical data collected exclusively in the port city.

This bipolar structure of port–provinces became consolidated, along with the country, during the nineteenth century with the shipment of raw materials to markets abroad, but not without a fierce struggle between *unitarios* and *federales*. As a matter of fact, the multiple forms of this same basic conflict of interests, which lasted throughout the twentieth century, would end up contained within the shifting boundaries of a single political party, Peronism. But before this happened, the debut of the import-substitution model of industralization (in which the state favored domestic production and domestic firms) in Argentina brought wave after wave of province dwellers to the port city of Buenos Aires. Discriminated against economically, politically, and culturally, these internal immigrants became the bedrock of this new political party.

The opposition between *unitarios* and *federales* and between anti-Peronists and Peronists embody the conflict between the port city of Buenos Aires and the rest of the country, a dichotomy that in Latin America as a whole is summed up by the formula "civilization and barbarousness." Thus, nationalizing in Argentina has historically meant Buenos Aires gaining hegemony over an area of the country or a sector of the population, or its converting a culturally diverse population generally considered inferior to the dominant culture. Territorially, nation building has implied fortifying land routes that follow the railroad lines to Buenos Aires, from where relations with the rest of the world are undertaken.

This type of territorialization began to change several decades back. For one thing, geopolitical strategy no longer sought to defend against neighboring countries; the idea instead was to join with them to form regional trading blocs. Also, transnational economic relations broadened, as regional entities tied into larger globalization processes increased in power at the expense of central government. And finally, approximately two decades of stability under democratically elected governments brought about some degree of federalization: provinces enjoyed more power than before, and policy making tended toward decentralization.

This complex policy trajectory lends itself to analysis from different, often conflicting points of view. In some cases, conditions existed that favored citizenship and civil society participation in territorial matters. But given the radical neoliberalism adhered to by Argentina in the 1990s, this decentralizing tendency can best be described as follows: the authoritarian, highly centralized model characterizing the prior stage was replaced by a neoliberal model that tended to encourage territorial reorganization in accordance with market interests. The term *market* is understood to mean, in this case, the most powerful economic agents positioned at the crossroads between productive development and global economic tendencies.

During the second half of the twentieth century, there was only one political border in the Southern Cone where war might break out: the one separating Argentina and Chile. During the nineteenth century any number of conflicts and several wars had taken place in the region. Río de Janeiro and Buenos Aires fought in the Río de la Plata region between 1825 and 1828; an alliance made up of Brazil, Argentina, and Uruguay made war on Paraguay from 1865 to 1870, and Chile fought Bolivia and Peru in the War of the Pacific between 1879 and 1884. The country of Uruguay came into being as a result of the first of the wars mentioned above; the second physically decimated the Paraguayan male population, and the third left Bolivia landlocked. In the twentieth century Bolivia and Paraguay fought the War of the Chaco between 1932 and 1935.

Argentine concern oscillated between its border with Brazil and the one with Chile. More difficult to reach and less populated, the latter one became the cornerstone of Argentina's "border policy." In some Argentine history books, the Patagonian border with Chile is treated as the paragon of frontiers, a throwback to the nineteenth-century Campaign of the Desert that depopulated this region of Indians and extended Argentina's southern frontier.

From time to time, one or another of the many unsettled border questions remaining between Argentina and Chile gained diplomatic or military importance. In the late 1970s tension over the Beagle Canal put the two countries on war footing. According to news stories published not long ago, Argentine troops actually reached the Chilean side of the Andes before the order to retreat that avoided war was given.

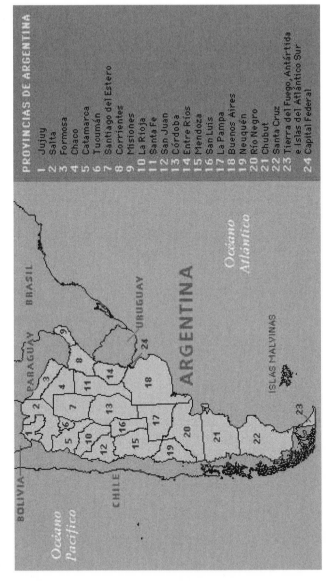

PROVINCIAS DE ARGENTINA

1 Jujuy
2 Salta
3 Formosa
4 Chaco
5 Catamarca
6 Tucumán
7 Santiago del Estero
8 Corrientes
9 Misiones
10 La Rioja
11 Santa Fe
12 San Juan
13 Córdoba
14 Entre Ríos
15 Mendoza
16 San Luis
17 La Pampa
18 Buenos Aires
19 Neuquén
20 Río Negro
21 Chubut
22 Santa Cruz
23 Tierra del Fuego, Antártida e Islas del Atlántico Sur
24 Capital Federal

Figure 1.1

27 **Territory, Nation and Mercosur**

Both countries had been preparing for war for decades, investing in infrastructure and installing public enterprises, means of communication, frontier schools, and military regiments along the disputed stretch of their common border. They also had land and antitank mines.

There were also problems along the Brazilian border, especially in the provinces of Corrientes and Misiones where Brazilian influence was strong. Argentina felt threatened by the advance of Brazilian hubs of development and highways, as well as the plans to build bridges across the River Uruguay and the so-called cultural penetration of the Brazilian mass media. Other signs of frontier consolidation on the part of Brazil such as increased contraband and local organizations for fomenting commerce and tourism also unnerved Argentine geopoliticians.

From the war scenario perspective, frontiers were danger zones where the Argentine presence needed to be fomented in some areas and consolidated in others. In Brazil the military elite that took power in the 1964 coup refloated the old idea of the national territory as the *Ilha Brasil,* an island isolated from its neighbors on its borders, and within them, an archipelago in need of integration. Domestically the emphasis was on internal integration, including expanding state presence in underdeveloped regions; externally the idea was to implement a policy of development that would create "living frontiers" along which there would be lively transborder interchanges.

The response to the growing Brazilian economic, demographic, and military superiority along common borders was a geopolitical alarm sounded in the 1970s by diplomats and the military on the Argentine side. According to them, the contrast could not be more stark. Through incompetence and simple neglect, Argentina had frittered away most of the territory it had inherited from the Viceroyalty of the Río de la Plata. Brazil, on the other hand, had multiplied again and again the narrow strip accorded it east of Tordesillas during colonial times. In the 1970s, in Argentine nationalists' eyes, Brazil had consolidated its influence over Paraguay and Bolivia, with Uruguay and even Peru within reach. And of course Argentina's difficult relations with Chile had to be taken into account. All in all, the nationalists saw Brazil's influence spreading and Argentina as increasingly isolated.

In this analysis Brazil's victory in the battle for regional hegemony had to be reversed quickly. It was in this context that the Argentine military put into practice the policy of "frontiers for development," involving both present and potential border dwellers and including social programs in pursuit of nationalist goals. A former director of the Superior School of War stated publicly in 1975 that, in time, war with Brazil might become a necessity.

During this stage, frontier policy combined a massive military presence with a "cultural" offensive involving new public schools and mass media outlets. Economic policy was mixed, with development being encouraged in some regions and discouraged in others. The rationale for the latter was that, to counter a Brazilian invasion from the River Uruguay, an empty strip with neither industry nor highways should be left in place as a potential battleground. Consequently the main cities and areas of economic development in Misiones and Corrientes, the two provinces between the rivers Uruguay and Paraná bordering Brazil, ended up located along the latter river.

Just as in a war, where retreating armies destroy their reserves to keep them out of enemy hands, not only was frontier development considered incompatible with national security but also Argentine and Brazilian train tracks have different gauges, and paved roads reached the River Uruguay only a short time ago. By the same token, the public-sector enterprises, army bases, mass media installations, and schools conceived tactically in the context of the war scenario are almost all found along the River Paraná.

Public-sector enterprises could also effectively act as defense installations. At the southern extreme of the continent, a little to the north of Tierra del Fuego, in the 1950s the Argentine government installed a coal mine—whose main purpose was to produce sovereignty, not coal—in an uninhabited region of the national territory. One of the obstacles the project faced was that few inhabitants of a developing country, which Argentina was at that time, were willing to brave the Patagonian winter. So, ironically enough, the actual coal miners turned out to be Chileans who migrated from a nearby poor region of their own country to produce sovereignty in Río Turbio, Argentina (Vidal 2000). When this territorialization model came to an end in the early 1990s, the Río Turbio coal mine was privatized.

Another interesting case occurred in the province of San Juan, midpoint on the long frontier separating Argentina and Chile. One of the primary patriotic tales on the founding of Argentina, taught to every Argentine child in primary school, is that José San Martín crossed the Andes to liberate Argentina, Chile, and Peru from Spain. This heroic feat is even more impressive, given the fact that the Andes have always been considered a *natural frontier* separating two economic systems and cultural identities (Escolar 2000). But, oblivious to this orographic barrier, local people traditionally ignored the existence of the frontier, crisscrossing at will, buying and selling or, more frequently, shepherding their flocks.

Beginning in the middle of the nineteenth century, local identity was marked by national and provincial governments that tended to reproduce the Argentine–Chilean dichotomy. But not until a highway was constructed between Calingasta and the provincial capital, the city of San Juan, in the 1920s did the presence of the state become concrete. The desire on the part of the Argentine provincial elite to establish sovereignty meant closer control of transfrontier traffic and the nationalization of the nomad population, whose economic links at the time were with Chile. An Argentine military presence was established in the 1940s with the construction of gendarme outposts in several foothill localities. Next, a campaign was launched to nationalize the frontier population in 1945. From then on national bonds were strengthened with expanded citizenship rights for border dwellers, as well as their proletarianization and participation in local development projects. In the 1990s the same highway that had symbolized integration into the Argentine nation for the local population was closed down for lack of repairs.

Both the military government that held power between 1966 and 1973 and the one that ruled from 1976 to 1983 dictated special frontier norms whose objective was "development and integration" (Law 18.575 and Law 19.524, Decree 2336). Economic and demographic weakness along its borders, they argued, made Argentina vulnerable. It was, therefore, imperative to "ensure the integration of these territories with the rest of the nation." To this end, the law "entailed protecting the territorial integrity of the nation by bringing about development in a frontier zone." This formula makes clear the key equation: "development" is a legitimate means of protecting "territorial integrity."

Social policy is a function of nationalization in the same way that nationalization is a function of "territorial integrity." In this sense, the principal means to these complementary ends can be listed as follows: settle, defend, stimulate development, integrate, Argentinize. Obtaining hegemony over and legitimacy in the eyes of frontier populations crucial for national security, this rationale raised the stature of frontier zones in domestic policy making, giving it a regionally oriented flavor. These policy measures were put into practice in October 1978, at a time when the major goals of state terrorism had been accomplished and tension with Chile was at its height.

State Terrorism and Operation Condor

That this particular social policy was implemented by the perpetrators of state terrorism is worthy of further comment. Clearly the social policy was authoritarian in nature. The idea was to impose new cultural patterns on frontier dwellers to turn them into cultural examples of the "prototypical Argentine" in the eyes of the military. And the regime that sought to achieve the territorial and sociocultural objective of frontier hegemony was the most repressive in the annals of Argentine history.

The other side of the war scenario coin was the growing cooperation among Southern Cone repressive forces. Operation Condor was a secret multinational force made up of armed forces and intelligence service members from Argentina, Chile, Uruguay, Brazil, Paraguay, and Bolivia. The objective was the exchange of information on persons sought for political reasons and their capture, assassination, or disappearance beyond the frontiers of their native country. Facilities were established for the clandestine movement and activity of these agents, and joint repressive operations were carried out. Special groups were also formed to intervene in different countries.[1]

Beginning in 1975 numerous Chilean political activists were detained in Argentina and Paraguay and turned over to the Chilean repressive forces. The most famous cases involved Uruguayans and Chileans kidnapped in Argentina or Brazil and Argentines captured in Brazil, as well as political leaders of these countries killed in Italy and Washington D.C. (in the case of O. Letelier). Joint operations grew during the rest of the decade. In October 1976 the Argentine military government requested collaboration from the Center of Information of the Brazilian Army in their search for 149 Argentines accused of "having practiced subversive acts" (*Clarín* May 21, 2000). Brazilian forces cooperated, and Argentine agents had no trouble moving around inside Brazil and capturing many of them.

This cooperation between military forces with a long history of mutual distrust marked the beginning of a change in the way Southern Cone countries viewed their neighbors. The specter of communism in the context of the cold war and the spread of national security doctrines constitute one chapter in the globalization and regionalization of Southern Cone political conflicts.

One regional frontier strategy employed by the Argentine military dictatorship targeted exiles. When people managed to cross a border, they ran a grave risk of being kidnapped or detained in the neighboring country. The other strategy, directed at incoming Argentines, was increased military control at the crossing points along the "disappearing frontiers." In the months following the coup in 1976, control had increased at departure points; in 1978 the Army concentrated part of its repressive force at entry points.

In preparation for the so-called counteroffensive, the left-oriented Montonero organization began to bring middle-level activists back into the country from abroad. In response the Army fortified its presence at various border crossing points. This clandestine control was knows as the "marker system." The markers, also known as "hard fingers," were guerrillas who, after having been kidnapped and tortured by the Army or the Navy, had allegedly agreed to collaborate with the military to save their life. Both the guerrilla organizations and the military referred to these collaborators as "broken." There were diverse ways of collaborating. The marker system consisted of taking "broken" militants to frontier crossing points and getting them to finger former comrades, who would then be detained and kidnapped, and then disappear.

The procedure was as follows: when a collaborator saw a former comrade entering or leaving the country, he would advise the on-duty official, who would detain the person. The prisoner would then usually be hooded and taken to a site where torture would begin.

When militants tried to cross the border into a neighboring country—as generation after generation of persons persecuted for political reasons before them had done and avoided being fingered by a marker on the frontier, they now had to face Operation Condor forces on the other side. State terrorism recognized no borders.

For more than a century juridical frontiers had been an important resource for escaping political persecution. Frontiers made a difference: on one side was persecution, and on the other, exile and safety. The difference could be between life and death. But when repressive forces began to coordinate efforts supranationally, frontiers were erased, as was any difference of treatment on one side or the other. The experience that military forces from Chile, Argentina, Uruguay, Paraguay, and Brazil gained during Operation Condor built up their "confidence" in each other. Thus, the first actual integration of Mercosur members was repressive in nature (see Boccia Paz 1999).

TOWARD REGIONAL INTEGRATION

The last military dictatorship in Argentina ended in 1983, at around the same time as other Southern Cone countries were also returning to constitutional government. A new global scenario, the growing weakness of military elites, and a new political orientation all combined to alter the direction of geopolitical strategy. In 1984 President Alfonsín called a plebiscite on whether to approve a peace treaty with Chile in which Argentina ceded on a territorial demand. The government's position was overwhelmingly approved, and since then diplomatic wheels have been set in motion to settle all pending border disputes. In 1985 Alfonsín and Brazilian president Sarney signed the Foz de Iguazú Declaration, which laid the foundation for integration between Brazil and Argentina.

With the signing of the Asunción Treaty in 1991, Mercosur came into being as a free-trade bloc made up of Argentina, Brazil, Paraguay, and Uruguay. Its main objective was integration based on the unfettered circulation of goods, services, and productive factors; the establishment of a common tariff and adoption of a common trade policy; the coordination of macroeconomic and sectorial policies; and the harmonization of legislation in pertinent areas.

In January 1995 Mercosur was officially born. From a purely economic perspective, Mercosur has been a success, but there are also serious problems. For example, compare

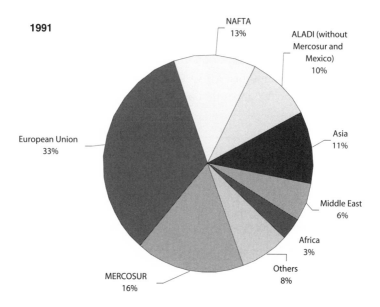

Figure 1.2

Destination of Mercosur country exports, 1991. (Source: *Boletín de Indicadores Socioeconómicas*, No. 99, subgrupo no. 14, Ministerio de Economía, Argentina.)

Mercosur country exports in 1991 and in 2001 in Figure 1.2 and Figure 1.3. The foreign trade indicator shows how trade with Latin America (excluding Mexico) went from 26 percent to 43 percent of total foreign trade in ten years. The evolution of total trade figures for Mercosur countries in the 1990s shows that whereas inter-Mercosur trade increased five times, trade with the rest of the world increased only two. It should be stated at this point that inter-Mercosur trade and international trade are two different worlds; in addition, although the former has decreased sharply since 1998, the latter has tended to stabilize.

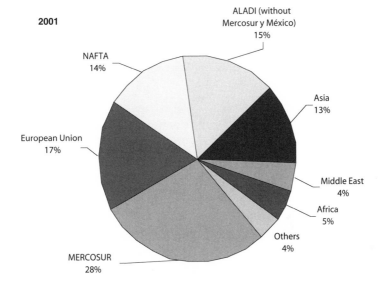

2001

ALADI (without Mercosur y México) 15%

NAFTA 14%

Asia 13%

European Union 17%

Middle East 4%

Africa 5%

Others 4%

MERCOSUR 28%

Figure 1.3
Destination of Mercosur country exports, 2001. (Source: *Boletín de Indicadores Socioeconómicas*, No. 99, subgrupo no. 14, Ministerio de Economía, Argentina.)

Since its inception, Mercosur has had a political dimension. To begin with, it marked the end of the war scenario era. The Asunción Treaty contains a clause according to which a coup in a member country can be cause for expulsion from Mercosur. On more than one occasion, diplomatic intervention by Argentina and Brazil has parried coup threats in Paraguay.

Unlike the European Union, however, Mercosur has no plans for developing supranational political institutions. A system does exist for consulting, forming commissions, and organizing forums and meetings between ministers and presidents. It is during the latter, of course, that final decision making takes place. But in the absence of any ceding of sovereignty to supranational institutions, macroeconomic coordination is out of the question. This obviously makes changes of economic direction by member countries impossible to foresee. As a result, when conflicts of interest arise, there is no regional arrangement for hammering out differences.

More than a decade after the signing of the Asunción Treaty, no one would dispute that the national interests of member countries prevail over any regional rationale in policy and practice. This is apparent in each nation's strategic policy. For example, Brazil has been seeking a permanent seat on the United Nation's Security Council, a campaign that Argentina has worked actively to thwart. This has generated deep resentment in both countries. Each country also negotiates on its own with international organizations like the International Monetary Fund, in accord with what it perceives as its national interests. Sometimes Brazil supports Argentina in times of high tension, and sometimes it does not. Also, agreements reached between presidents do not always hold up in the long run.

On the strictly regional plane, every macroeconomic imbalance—devaluation first in Brazil and then in Argentina or recession in one or the other country—has produced a temporary increase in certain imports or exports, setting off a sectorial crisis with diplomatic repercussions in one of the two countries. Warnings about the "invasion" of Brazilian, or Argentine, products then become common coin, and restrictive measures violating the basic tenets of a free-trade bloc are put into effect.

On some occasions these measures have included sanitary controls. An eloquent example was the foot-and-mouth disease crisis with cattle. When Argentina was declared "free of foot-and-mouth disease" in the late 1990s, barriers were immediately erected to keep out Brazilian cattle. Later on, when the disease reappeared in northern Argentina and southern Brazil, it was the latter country that shut its border to Argentine cattle. The throwing up of sanitary barriers was accompanied on both sides of the border by nationalistic rhetoric to the effect that "our country"—read Argentina, Brazil, and also Chile or Uruguay—is more "advanced" than its neighbors, so it must protect itself to keep foreign markets open to its products. On no occasion has a regional approach to a problem that obviously recognizes no borders even been mentioned.

The upshot is that the defense of corporate interests has tended to be framed in nationalist terms. Especially in times of crisis, regional solutions are never explored; instead, fires are stoked for the zero-sum game of throwing up frontier barriers and setting up extra-tariff mechanisms. In the worst case, trade disputes turn into veritable trade wars that awaken the war paranoia of the 1960s.

As we show next, this is related to a general tendency: Mercosur has tried to activate "integration from above," while at the same time generating down below new frontiers between populations and citizens.

NEOLIBERAL INTEGRATION

We are now going to change the angle of analysis. What better place to study the interaction between two states and two societies than down on the ground in a border zone? One might think that, with the reduction of artificial barriers between two countries, the first beneficiaries of Mercosur's integration policies would be border dwellers. Nothing could be further from the truth. As we show, once the war scenarios that were the rationale for government policy in frontier zones disappeared, so did the social programs. For their part, customs barriers were removed only for large companies; everyday citizens have faced more customs and immigration controls than ever.

Thus two complementary tendencies are found in frontier zones. On one hand, the state has implemented regulations and strengthened its control along key borders (see Karasik 2000; Grimson 2000a). And on the other, the "welfare" programs associated with the nationalization-through-social-policy model have all but disappeared (Escolar 2000; Vidal 2000).

In the mid-twentieth century a formula appeared that combined militaristic ends with certain processes for the "territorial and social integration" of frontier populations. "Welfare" was a means of nationalizing, which, in turn, would strengthen the nation in a war that, fortunately, never was fought. Beginning in the early 1990s, "regional integration" projects like Mercosur have replaced war scenarios on national agendas. But instead of bringing about a reappraisal of frontiers as a place for dialogue and interaction, the new priority has resulted in the abandoning of all programs for social development in frontier zones. Just as "welfare" coexisted with conflict, "integration" now coexists with neoliberalism.[2]

On one hand, public enterprises and military detachments are no longer projected as ways of settling frontier zones (see Vidal 2000). Projects to attract settlers to border areas by building roads, schools, and the like, which were firmly anchored in the war scenario model, have come to an end in many regions. New highways and bridges do not seek to benefit border dwellers, as was the case before. Now the rationale is to further interregional land trade by turning cities at border crossing points into "service zones" that provide the facilities needed for the circulation of mass-produced goods.

On the other hand, the control exercised over frontier populations appears to have increased, with regard to the circulation of both persons and petty or "ant" contraband. In 1998 the Argentine government established new regulations for local cross-border traffic that had a strange effect on the daily life of border dwellers. Since 1986 frontier inhabitants had been permitted to spend a maximum of US$150 *a day* in the neighboring border city. In late 1998 the rules changed: local residents could spend only US$100 *a month* on the other side of the border, less than the amount permitted a tourist. By reducing the cross-border purchasing power of middle- and lower-class border dwellers—traditional salary-stretchers who seek out the best price—the change made a big difference. Also seriously affected were the so-called passers, poor men and women who had eked out a living selling cross-border goods for slightly more than they paid for them.

From the state's point of view (i.e., favoring regional integration), the new regulation makes no sense, especially after eight years in Mercosur. Actually, the measure was a result of lobbying on the part of Argentine merchants in border cities. And after years of pressure strongly tinged with nationalistic rhetoric, they have recovered an almost captive market (see Grimson 2000a, 2003).

Because of more rigorous customs controls, crossing the border between Argentina and Brazil or Paraguay can now take several hours. Clearly, in the eyes of border dwellers, the state's role of protector has given way to that of enforcer of controls and regulations.

Along many other Southern Cone frontiers, demilitarization has been followed by stricter controls over the circulation of merchandise, people, and symbols. One example of the latter is the trouble Bolivian migrants and border dwellers had exporting and importing Carnaval costumes; another is the overzealous, nationalist-tinged rhetoric of Brazilian, Uruguayan, and Argentine sanitary officials who, during the foot-and-mouth disease crisis, disinfected both animals and people from the other side of the border.

The state has not withdrawn from frontier zones—rather the nature of state intervention has changed. If during the prior phase it was obsessed with the static preservation and control of national territory, its present-day concern is, essentially, to promote the large-scale cross-border flow of goods and services and keep a tight rein on the small-scale flows of goods and people.

The highway connecting Calingasta and the capital city of the province of San Juan mentioned previously is a case in point. In early 1998 the highway that, in its day, symbolized the incorporation of the region into the nation-state was closed down for lack of repairs. This closure "is interpreted locally as the virtual abandonment of the population and territory of Calingasta by a national government that is retracting the provision of the goods, services and perspectives that were once used to seduce the local population into becoming Argentine citizens" (Escolar, 2000, 274). Especially during military governments, because of the role played by frontier areas in sovereignty issues, frontier zone residents received benefits from the state. This is why closing the highway in 1998 represents a lack of interest in sovereignty over Calingasta and its residents, who were made *citizens* by the welfare-state-type benefits they no longer receive.

According to Escolar (2000), Argentinization had accompanied the local version of the "welfare state," which led local residents to abandon indigenous identifications, while the local version of neoliberalism has brought about a renewed interest in ethnic identity. Once considered extinct, the Wharpes have set up their own organizations in the public sphere.

The fate of the state-run coal mine in Río Turbio is also pertinent in this regard. In the early 1990s it was privatized; the state withdrew from a company town where the coal miners had been "soldiers doing their patriotic duty" mining coal. The switch from producing for the domestic economy under state control to producing for the global marketplace under private control played havoc with the complex identities and antagonisms forged in half a century of geopolitical confrontation between Argentina and Chile (Vidal 2000). Two social conflicts occurred in the town of Río Turbio in the 1990s. In 1994 Argentine and Chilean workers stood together in opposition to the labor practices of the privatized company. In sharp contrast, in 1997 Argentine inhabitants struggled alone in a town where the Chilean inhabitants and Chile had totally disappeared from the local political arena. In the course of three years the "meaning of the frontier and the relation between frontier and nation" had been totally transformed. The 1997 conflict was not with "the other from outside but rather the relationship of belonging between Argentines living on the frontier and the nation." It began when the Argentine residents of Río Turbio perceived that without state support for frontier development, they were being turned into outsiders or *chilotes,* whom they had been taught to place on the lowest rung of the social ladder and consider enemies.

In contrast to Río Turbio, where the state is withdrawing, in Northern Argentina border controls appear to have become more rigorous in recent years, at least for frontier zone residents. In this context of ever-tighter control, new dynamics of interchange and interaction have also given rise to new fears and tensions. In 1990 a bridge joining the Argentine city of Posadas with the Paraguayan one of Encarnación was inaugurated. Local actors and government officials from both countries celebrated the opening of the new viaduct as a symbol of "Latin American integration" and as "the end of frontiers between peoples." Nevertheless, the qualitative factor involved in the increase of persons, automobiles, and merchandise crossing the border unleashed disputes between different social sectors. The facility with which Posada residents could now shop in Encarnación and the traditional Paraguayan *paseras*—women who for more than a century had made a living selling their wares on the Argentine side—could now crisscross the frontier affected the interests of Posada merchants. Diverse organizations began to demand stricter customs control, alleging that Argentine currency crossing the bridge was fomenting the informal economy in Paraguay. The accusation heard in private was that the bridge had brought about "the economic debacle of the city." Stricter controls were then imposed, which, along with mistreatment by Argentine customs officials, unleashed a series of protests on the part of Paraguayan *paseras* and taxi drivers beginning in 1992. As tension between the frontier towns and Argentina and Paraguay grew, local, provincial, and national government officials began to get in on the act, and the conflict figured on the agenda of negotiations between the Argentine and Paraguay presidents (Grimson 1998). Partial measures enacted since then have done little to abate tension, and the conflict continues to this day.

The view of regionalization and the impact of integration policies is very different in the metropolis from what it is in frontier zones. Mercosur has planned for the future creation of a bi-ocean corridor as the rationale for constructing highways and bridges. At the national and binational level, paving highways and building bridges imply progress toward the twin goals of connecting countries and uniting peoples. But on the ground in frontier zones, reality is heterogeneous and therefore complex. Although the new bridges do speed up the movement of goods and people, to the degree that they favor commerce at the expense of petty contraband and the informal economy, they can be viewed as not uniting everyone. On the contrary, the subsequent reorganization of circulation patterns can lead to the bridge being viewed as the cause of new divisions, rancor, and disputes. And when implicated in the hardening of frontier controls, a bridge can end up separating the two sides of the river (Grimson 1998).

Another interesting example of how a river functions is found on the Argentine–Paraguayan frontier of the middle Pilcomayo River. When the frontier between the two countries was drawn along the Pilcomayo, a problem arose: because of the geographic characteristics of the region, the river would periodically change course. What was considered at one time the "main branch" a few years later would dry up. Not only did the meandering of the main branches of the river cause floods and droughts but the international frontier also constantly changed place, calling into question the concept of a natural frontier for separating two countries. In fact the different groups of people living along the river, mainly Tobas and

Wichis, also used the river for demarcation purposes, but in a different sense: instead of referring to one side or the other, they differentiated between "up river" and "down river." As military detachments multiplied and the state appeared in the area, the perception of the native people changed. In some cases they began to define intertribal limits according to where the international frontier ran (Gordillo and Leguizamón 2002).

In recent years two important public works projects have been carried out in the region. On one hand, the river has been channeled to avoid periodic floods and droughts, clarifying the "international boundary" at the same time. On the other, the consolidation of Mercosur has accelerated the process of overcoming physical obstacles to integration by building a bridge across the Pilcomayo, but without roads connecting it to anyplace else at the present time. For Gordillo and Leguizamón, this dual process of delimiting and uniting intertwines global, regional, national, and local processes. The indigenous population has been strongly involved, and the bridge has been built on the tribal land of one community. But the Indians decided to stop with the bridge and cede no more land, because nobody had consulted them about entering the global era. In fact, "the construction of the bridge and the arrival of Mercosur to the area were closely linked to the problem of land in the eyes of the indigenous groups," as was clearly shown when an indigenous leader stated, "I don't believe Mercosur is good for us because it tramples on us." Once again, borders were made flexible to facilitate the movement of capital, while "a greater control of the frontier on the part of state organisms" has had a restrictive effect on the local population.

The other side of the Mercosur coin has been a policy of flexibilization for transnational companies. With the signing of the Mercosur accord, the International Manifest of Cargo/Customs Crossing Declaration (IMC/CCD), an agreement that facilitates freight hauling by land between countries, came into being. International commerce has been speeded up because goods can be sent directly to their destination. Instead of stopping at customs and unloading so cargo can be checked, then waiting for dispatching paperwork to be completed when crossing from one Mercosur country to another, with an IMC/CCD, sealed cargo containers pass through customs without stopping on their way to large urban centers like Buenos Aires. The IMC/CCD has made border crossing very simple for international freight. The only customs checkpoint is the final destination of the load—Buenos Aires, for example. This saves time, which of course means money is saved. Thus it is fair to say that for multinational corporations, frontiers have disappeared.

These changes have modified the economic and political relevance of frontiers. Unlike the European Union, for example,[3] the move toward integrated trading blocs like Mercosur has reduced the importance of frontier zones as places where interaction and dialogue take place; they have been devalued to the point of becoming nothing more than places that international cargoes pass through. The loss of jobs and public funds has been made worse by the severe drop in the number of stevedores and customs dispatchers in cities that used to live off of international commerce and public funding for the purpose of getting people to perform their patriotic duty and live there. No projects for turning frontier zones into outposts for integration have been proposed; they have been abandoned to market forces in the interest of globalization.

Mercosur and its territorial imagery produce a new framework and a new rhetoric. Nevertheless, without some kind of supranational political apparatus qua national state, Mercosur will not produce specific benefits in frontier zones, and it will not broaden the concept of citizenship, incorporate excluded sectors of the population, or acquire the institutional attributes of genuine indeterminacy. At present, Mercosur is merely a facilitator of demands that frontier populations and interest groups make of their own provincial and national government officials. Indeed, the very existence of frontiers increases competition between Mercosur-member-country residents living on either side. This is why national identities tend to be strengthened, not erased.

THE INVENTION OF "MERCOSURNESS" AS CULTURAL POLICY

A characteristic common to neoliberal cultural policy has been the attempt to turn economic losses into cultural profit. An eloquent example in several Latin American countries has been the tendency of the sustained rise in socioeconomic inequality to be accompanied by an increased recognition on the cultural plane of the right to be different. In Chile research has pointed up the paradox between women's success in gaining recognition and asserting their legal rights and the growing inequality in their earning power when compared with men's.

Mercosur has attempted to do the same thing. Politicians, intellectuals, and academics have sought to design a cultural policy that will establish a top-down common identity in member countries. In the absence of any increase in concrete rights—regional advantages for member-country citizens, for example—or any long-term project for regional political sovereignty, bureaucratic creativity has been the order of the day.

Seminars have been called that were attended by high-ranking foreign ministry officials and leading intellectuals from member countries; progress has been made in formulating teaching material for schools; and some cultural and educational accords have been signed. But because of the lack of any common identity in the present-day world, the only alternative has been to reach into the past. One possibility—the reworking from a regional perspective of the great conflicts in member countries' history—was rejected in favor of common narratives whose unreality approaches that of absurdity.

One example is the identification of Mercosur with the Jesuit missions on the basis of the existence of their ruins in Brazil, Argentina, and Paraguay. Historically the missions served the Spanish Crown as, among other things, a human and military frontier against the advance of the Portuguese from the south and west. For their part, mission Indians resisted both the Portuguese advance and the Spanish attempt to turn them into a workforce for Spaniards. Spain and Portugal then united, following the signing of a border treaty in 1750. The Guaraní opposed the treaty because it left seven Guaraní settlements in Portuguese territory (present-day Brazil). They went to war and were defeated. So linking the Jesuit missions with the idea of the ancestral brotherhood of Latin American peoples is nothing short of absurd.

It should be noted, however, that cultural policy, and not "academic" error, is responsible for anecdotes such as those previously mentioned. The stated aim is finding an integrationist angle from which to fabricate a romantic tale of past "brotherhood" among Mercosur member peoples. A series of research projects and essays have sought to legitimize the integration process historically, geographically, and culturally (see Recondo 1997; Clementi 1996; AA.VV 1997a). Recondo (1997) proposed "implementing a suitable cultural policy and strategy for redefining our collective identity based on our differences and developing, together with our MERCOSUR brothers." Clementi (1996) saw in Mercosur a field "where a new *American, mestizo, peculiar, authentic* spirit was growing and spreading out over virgin land" (italics in original). Within this framework, he proposed the development of a historiography based on "our common reality and history to legitimize the construction of a future in which the Cultural MERCOSUR will be the foundation for its relevance and projection" (1996, 43).

This integrationist perspective seeks out historical moments in common, bypassing the nationalistic perspective found in member-country history books. By recovering these moments, the foundation is laid for a community whose existence is based on "becoming conscious of" or "accepting" a set of cultural peculiarities denied in the past. Mercosur is seen as an opportunity for forging a unity that did not exist at the time it came into existence. In other words, *thinking of and projecting regional unity* could also be a way of forming new alliances and support for national economic, political, and cultural recognition.

An example of one supranational identity engineering project is the "Cultural, Social and Economic Atlas of Mercosur" (AA.VV 1997a). Its publication is relevant because of the support it received from the Cultural Ministry of Brazil, along with Petrobras as a sponsor and a number of important regional intellectuals as collaborators. Composed of graphs, maps, and articles by authors with diverse orientations, the atlas appears to be an early example of projecting Mercosur as a "subregional culture" or the "cultural spirit of Mercosur." Two key issues are resolved by redefining historical, temporal, and special factors to project a new image of the region: a "peninsular alliance" is posited on the basis of the invasion of Portugal and sixty years of domination over it in the sixteenth and seventeenth centuries, and a teleology is assumed according to which subsequent problems paved the way for the present integration process (AA.V 1997a).

Authors thus dutifully comply with the order issued by the Argentine vice chancellor to notable historians in a seminar: history should be written from the present. In making the case for history as instrumental to integration, the vice chancellor affirmed that because "the past is not neutral," it is urgently important to seek out "the roots of coincidences that will strengthen the project of a convergent future" (Cisneros 2000, 392). As "the view of the present inevitably conditions how we end up seeing the past," it is necessary to "look for and identify the threads leading to a cooperative present" (Cisneros 2000, 394). This summons was not explicitly responded to until 1999, when Hilda Sábato and Adrián Gorelik refused the invitation to write a functional or operative history. They stated that, clearly, "the *questions* we ask the past are strongly marked by the climate of ideas in the moment of asking them." They added that it is necessary, however, that "this climate limit the *answers* as much as possible; otherwise, the work of the historian would be pointless" (Sábato 2000, 709). That "history can only be written from the present" does not deny that, when posed by the political power structure, "seeking to influence the historian's work, … it is nothing short of an attempt to operatively appropriate intellectual work, and as such, it is worrisome"

(Gorelik 2000, 26). History should serve no other specific purpose than the objective of writing the best history possible (Gorelik 2000, 726).

The efforts toward historical engineering had a correlate in the new spatial boundaries perceived to establish a supposed "territorial fusion." In the atlas a new world map is drawn up organized around regional trading blocs (see "Nuevo mapamundi con el Mercosur en el centro del mundo," in AA.VV. 1997a, 158–59), as well as a new "political map of South America" using four different colors: one for the four Mercosur countries, one for the two countries associated with it, one for the four nonassociated countries, and the last for the Guyanas (p. 24). The same criterion is used in drawing up Mercosur maps of agricultural production, transportation, mining productions, consumer goods, and interconnections between Mercosur countries, among others.

We should mention that these positions were criticized at the time. In a paper criticizing both the nationalism that put obstacles in the way of integration and the "laudatory view" of the latter, Denise Leite (1994) questioned how the historical differences and distrust dating back to colonial times will fit into this process, as well as the stereotypes of Brazilian women, ethnic origins, military schools, expansionist ideas in Brazil viewed as imperialistic by neighboring countries, and the supposed transborder linguistic invasion by television and satellite. In a word, Leite pointed out the existence of sociocultural and historical differences and problems that were neither diluted nor resolved when the Asunción Treaty was signed. In 1997, in the same seminar, a group of intellectuals proposed establishing a space for dialogue, instead of inventing props for integration: rather than inventing regional identity, generating dialogue; rather than integration, discussing interaction.

MERCOSUR VIEWED FROM NATIONAL HINTERLANDS

Just as globalization has not spelled the end of the nation-state, Mercosur has not erased frontiers. Instead states and their political frontiers have been transformed. The objective of the new policies is not primarily one of controlling territory or nationalizing populations; it is circulation. If until the end of the war scenario era in the mid-1980s the concerns of Southern Cone nations centered around preserving their own territory, the tendency toward "regional integration," which fortunately has put an end to geopolitical bad dreams, has opened the way for a new kind of competition. States have shifted their policy concerns and now emphasize the circulation of capital, goods, and people. The key is no longer space but flow.

Far from leading to unrestricted cooperation among nation-states, the desire to increase international trade behind common-market-type trading blocs has changed the framework of and rules of play for competition between them. During the recurring crisis and economic difficulties of recent years, states have sought to adjust, strengthen, or flexibilize frontiers in accordance with disputes regarding real and potential import and export flows. In a framework dominated by the rationale of "national interest"—more often than not a euphemism for the export or captive market interests of large companies—policies designed to benefit broader social sectors have been passed over.

Thus, an economic scenario has replaced the war scenario, and flexibility for large-scale international commerce has had as counterpart an increasingly rigorous control over traditional informal flows of goods and services. Where frontier populations once interacted spontaneously, strict customs checkpoints now exist. With Mercosur, the traditional practice of saving money by cross-border shopping has become illegal. State presence along frontiers has changed. It is a question not of installing Army regiments or intelligence service offices—although in some cases they continue functioning—but rather of establishing and putting into practice new rules of play for commerce and institutions.

Control over the frontier is reaffirmed by converting the former emphasis on military measures to ever-greater fiscal control. The former monopoly over violence within national boundaries has been replaced by a monopoly over tax revenue that characterizes any and all states.

During the 1990s this fiscal control had socioeconomic repercussions (see chapters 2 and 3). In fact, cross-border commerce reaches far beyond the border. The *passadores,* petty smugglers whose activity is termed "ant" contraband, are the central hub of a transnational network that dates back more than a century. The political singularity of this network is that it exists outside state control, thus evading its fiscal monopoly. Tax evasion, along with an ability to profit from minimal rational price differences, is the economic key to the success of a system operated by petty smugglers who transport products consumed by popular sectors from one side of the frontier to cities far from the border on the other. Indeed, tax evasion is the way that vast social sectors increase their purchasing power. The frontier and frontier crossers play a key role in this process.

The new integration policies are attempting to do away with traditional forms of informal exchange like the one described earlier. States that had an eminently military and geopolitical presence along their borders during integration now began to exert an unprecedented control over frontier populations and their economic practices. Control over frontier zones has been reaffirmed, but with a change in emphasis from military to fiscal control. The strategic importance in former decades of the monopoly over violence inside borders has reappeared in the form of states needing to defend their fiscal monopoly.

This explains why Mercosur is perceived at the frontier as yet another chapter of separation from and confrontation with the state. In other words, on the frontier Mercosur is viewed as exactly the opposite of what the political image makers had in mind: a foreign presence. Mercosur can be perceived as "alien" by a *passador:* "Mercosur are those truckloads of things going that way" or "Mercosur is the prohibition to keep us from crossing with merchandise." It also can be perceived as a key case of severe problems: the increase in unemployment, the closing of customs dispatcher offices, and border restrictions.

In another context, local social actors may use their geographic location to enhance their relevance to Mercosur—border cities, for instance, frequently refer to themselves as in "the heart of Mercosur." But in all likelihood, this sort of rhetoric is merely cover for demands by such cities for more resources from local, provincial, or federal government officials.

In no case is Mercosur perceived as directly benefiting frontier dwellers, and it is not viewed as broadening the notion of citizenship, incorporating marginal sectors of the population, or generating beneficial institutions. It is therefore impossible to affirm that, at this time, Mercosur has the kind of supranational political or cultural identity that could be considered in the same light as the political and cultural identity of the nation, which reorganized local and provincial identity patterns. And indications are that the supranational dimension of Mercosur will remain just one more element in a context of ongoing social and political dispute for a long time to come.

Mercosur has not wiped out old stereotypes and identificatory mechanisms of its different members. The new context and interaction it has brought in its wake seem to indicate a recycling of the meaning of and boundaries for differentiation and regrouping that do not necessarily coincide with "Mercosurness" and that, in many cases, exacerbate existing distinctions and conflicts at the national level. This is linked to the fact that the benefits of "neoliberal integration" have been limited to certain economic sectors, the same sectors in whose benefit member states put into practice policies and measures in the name of "the national interest." To comprehend the process, we need an analysis of the main economic and social transformations brought about by neoliberalism in Argentina in particular, and the Southern Cone in general.

*I had heard talk about Argentina, many of our people had
come back and commented in the village that they were
fine, that they had bought a house, that they had set up
businesses and that they were doing well, very well indeed.
It was a very rich country, they said, like the United States
but even richer. ... When I heard this I began to think
and think, I looked at the village, I looked at the poverty,
I imagined something else, and I began to think why not,
why not go too. ...*

On March 25, 1916, Adolfo Torrentanto arrived at the port of
Buenos Aires on the ship *Magenta*, which had left Genoa almost
a month before. Except for this interview in 1955, nothing more
is known about him. More than likely, he was just one more of
the five million immigrants from Spain, Italy, Poland, Uruguay,
Germany, Syria, Bolivia, Chile, Russia, Peru, Hungry, and Armenia,
among others, who, from the mid-nineteenth century on, chose
to live in Argentina. In light of this man's testimony, one can
only wonder what his destiny was and what became of his early
hopes and dreams, based as they were on the image of a rich
country offering opportunity and social mobility.

With more than 50 percent of all Argentines living below the
poverty line as the new millennium began, the obvious question
now is what happened to the country that, not so many decades
ago, attracted immigrants from around the world by offering

salaries, social rights, and levels of integration unmatched in the region. Paraphrasing Juan Carlos Torre, Argentina was a society whose social and political dynamics expressed "a passion for equality." But then again, the turnabout was neither unexpected nor sudden; instead, it was the result of long decades of social, political, and economic decline that gradually destroyed one kind of society and created another.

This is, of course, not a strictly Argentine phenomenon. It is rather a regional process that began with the military dictatorships that devastated the Southern Cone in the 1970s and continued on through the economic ups and downs of democratic governments during the so-called Lost Decade of the 1980s, when economic growth stopped. Next came a series of neoliberal reforms applied, to a greater or lesser degree, throughout the Southern Cone during the 1990s, reforms that, if not originating in the economic globalization process, were certainly accentuated by it. In Argentina this series of events "destructured" the century-old social imagery of a more egalitarian Argentina, the social dynamics of which had been destroyed. "This isn't the same country," members of the impoverished middle class state again and again. But if truth be told, this perturbing "other country" is the logical outcome of a long process begun decades earlier that finally erupted in their daily lives.

To understand present-day Argentina, we take a close look at the culminating moments of this long period of decline. The free trade and deindustrialization policies imposed by the military dictatorship, followed by the hyperinflation that undid the first democratically elected government that succeeded it, opened the way for the far-reaching neoliberal reform process that took place in the 1990s. We explore these two preparatory periods in the present chapter and place emphasis on the relationship between government policy and social thought. Argentina characterized each policy program as paradigmatic for the problems posed at the time, putting the legitimate steps that could be taken to resolve them.

DEINDUSTRIALIZATION POLICY

The so-called import-substitution model of industrialization appeared in the 1930s when Argentine raw materials no longer found a market in Europe because of the Great Depression. This meant Argentina could no longer exchange its raw materials—the meat and wheat from its fertile Pampa grasslands—for manufactured goods, its initial integration into the world market. A two-stage industrialization process followed. The first stage, which peaked during Peron's first government (1946–55), concentrated on producing basic consumer goods; the second, which began with the presidency of A. Frondizi (1958–62), was based on heavy industry and consumer goods for the middle and upper classes. Although recurrent structural problems led to cyclical balance of payment crises right from the start, this particular model remained at the heart of Argentine social dynamics until the last military dictatorship took power in 1976.

The reasons for putting an end to the import-substitution model of development were profoundly ideological, resulting from the coming together of the authoritarianism of the armed forces and the liberal tenets of their economist allies. According to L.A. Romero (1994), from the military government's perspective, prior wielders of political power had lacked the strength necessary to adequately deal with the two main corporate interest groups in Argentina—organized workers and the private-sector entrepreneurs who benefited from a protectionist state. The outcome of the confrontation between them was chronic political and social disorder as well as chaos and endemic inflation. Viewed in this light, the solution was political and social in nature: the corporate actors had to be disciplined at all cost, even if this meant sacrificing economic development. Once order was restored and the body politic well organized, the stage would be set for orderly economic development.

Ever present in the discourse of the power structure during these years was the authoritarian metaphor of a sick body under attack from disruptive factors such as labor unions and leftist (or simply progressive) forces such as student groups and intellectuals—in sum, any group or individual stressing conflict where homogeneity and consensus should reign supreme. The social and economic imagery of the times followed this lead. While political repression decimated the leadership of political parties and labor unions, as well as any and all opposing voices, economic policy set about dismantling the material foundations of the preexisting economic and social order. To this end the financial sector was reformed, trade liberalized, and salaries reduced. The stated objective of these policies was to modernize the economy and increase the competitiveness of a productive sector long pampered by protectionism. Far from achieving these objectives, these policies when put into effect devastated the Argentine economy: one of the worst economic crises ever in Argentine industry began in the early 1980s, which also marked the onset of the foreign debt crisis that has conditioned economic policy from that day to now (See Canitrot 1979, Schvarzer 1986).[1]

The 1982 foreign debt crisis in Argentina, following on the heels of Mexico's debt crisis, had a negative impact throughout

Latin America. The military's economic strategy became increasingly shaky, and in the context of incipient social discontent, the government launched an attempt to retake the Falkland Islands. This led to war with Great Britain, interrupting centuries of pacific dispute over the sovereignty of the islands. It was a last-ditch attempt to bring the nation together in the face of an increasingly severe economic crisis. Following the Argentine defeat, democracy was restored. The economic policy of Raúl Alfonsín, the democratically elected Argentine president who took office in 1983, was marked by its unsuccessful fight against inflation. As the government appeared less and less able to control the situation, the image of an inefficient, wasteful "elephantine State," which was repeated again and again in the media by economic liberals, fixed itself in public opinion. This time around, the solution to decades of economic instability was to privatize Argentina's public-sector enterprises and exercise strict monetary control.

These reforms, among others, were put into practice some years later, but the novelty at this point was that liberal preaching on reducing the size of the state—"Reduce the State to Aggrandize the Nation" appeared as a bumper sticker at the time—began for the first time ever to gain popularity in Argentine society at large. In the place of the stereotyped image of an inefficient, bureaucratic state there began to emerge the picture of a streamlined, agile one, whose business mentality and objective of "more and more efficiency" would benefit all Argentines.

POVERTY AND HUNGER MAKE THEIR PUBLIC DEBUT

Inflation wasn't the only problem that played havoc with the illusions raised by the return of democracy. The political instability that came in the wake of recurrent military uprisings to avoid being brought to trial for crimes committed during the preceding dictatorship was also profoundly unsettling. Still another, albeit less visible, factor was the airing of social problems in public. Prohibited during the military dictatorship, the social research carried out after the return of democracy depicted a very different country from the one Argentines had imagined they lived in for so long. In the new Argentina, around a third of the population lived below the poverty line as a result of the economic policies in effect during the dictatorship and the severe recession that followed in the 1980s. The figures on poverty in 1985 came as a shock to Argentines, who thought of hunger as something that occurred in far away countries or, closer to home, in Latin American countries that had little in common with Argentina. In this context Raúl Alfonsín launched the National Nutritional Plan (PAN), thus placing the problem of hunger in the public sphere, where it has remained ever since.

Although social welfare is considered natural today, people were shocked when the Alfonsín government began handing out food. For decades, labor laws had included provisions providing indirect income for wage earners; persons not covered by these laws could count on a network of public hospitals for health care, as well as other state-provided benefits in case of an emergency. However, for all practical purposes, this was the first time that food had been distributed by the state on a regular basis—around 700,000 families received PAN boxes (Hintze 1986). This innovation was by no means insignificant, given the fact that it flew in the face of the classic representation of a worker's "dignity" resting on his breadwinning capacity. In addition, because unemployment was relatively low at the time, it stands to reason that many

PAN recipients did work from time to time. But, because of the steep depreciation of wage earners' purchasing power, they could no longer feed their families on what they earned. According to research on the new poverty profile, there was cultural resistance to receiving the handouts on the part of some eligible middle-class members, who steadfastly refused the PAN boxes, even in cases of dire necessity. They alleged that the boxes were meant for the "truly poor," by which they meant people unable to feed and dress their family on what they earned (Kessler 1998).[2]

Another change brought to light by the PAN program was the new topography of social conflict. It was implicitly recognized that poverty had spread geographically. No longer a problem limited to poor provinces in the north of Argentina, the map now included greater Buenos Aires, not so long ago known as the scene of labor conflicts over wages, not as a place where people went hungry. In a PAN text dating from 1984, whose racial connotations are surprising, the new topography was described as follows: "Poverty is found not only as a *dense dark stain* in poor provinces, but also within the limits of greater Buenos Aires."[3] Nevertheless, severely restrained by the Alfonsín government's limited view of the role of government, the PAN program was viewed as a strictly emergency measure designed to bridge the gap until the economic recovery and the income redistribution that was inevitable in a democracy kicked in. In the policy papers on which the program was based, it is described as a measure designed to assist the "innocent victims" of the military government's economic policy. There, too, the consensus for the illusion of hunger as a transitory, even anomalous, phenomenon appeared. Obviously, the new poverty profile had not even made a dent in Argentine social imagery, which remained intact. In hindsight, however, the PAN program is clearly a milestone: it marked the first official recognition of the severe impoverishment that had occurred in Argentina.

HYPERINFLATION AND THE DISSOLUTION OF THE SOCIAL BOND[4]

After two years of democratic euphoria, social discontent became increasingly pronounced in response to runaway inflation.[5] It was in this context that Alfonsín announced a "war economy" in 1985, going on to say that "the institution of money has vanished in Argentina." After the launching of the "Austral Plan," the inflation rate became the one and only criterion for evaluating government performance. And monetary stability, once the exclusive province of right-wing ideologues, became the foremost priority for Argentines across the political spectrum. It had achieved the level of "common sense."

Hyperinflation came two years later in 1989. Although falling short of the great hyperinflationary crises of the twentieth century (the closest ones in time and space being the Bolivian crisis of 1985 and the Peruvian one of 1990),[6] it is generally accepted that hyperinflation engulfed Argentina in February 1989. In point of fact, the perspective of a Peronist victory in the presidential election scheduled for May 1989 led speculators to dump the peso and buy dollars; this, in conjunction with financial maneuvering to bring down the Alfonsín government, led the Central Bank to stop selling foreign currency, and three months later the Argentine peso had lost 100 percent of its value. But already in April, in response to the monetary chaos reigning at the time, the Argentine Business Federation stated that "no clear rules exist for the functioning of either the marketplace or prices," a situation the daily newspaper *Clarín* characterized by "price lists that last less than a day, the lack of reference values for renewing stock, limited distribution, products being bought with US dollars, the disappearance of any and all financing." In early June the combination of runaway prices and empty shelves triggered unprecedented looting and confrontations, especially in working-class neighborhoods.

Above and beyond its economic significance, hyperinflation marked a point of no return in recent Argentine history. Diverse testimonies recorded at the time attest to Argentines viewing their country as on the brink of social dissolution. Whether the perception was warranted, politically hyperinflation marked the end of the democratic illusions inspired by Alfonsín, who had based a large part of his campaign on the idea that democracy meant an end to social problems. Arising out of the dichotomy between democracy and authoritarianism that had generated wide acceptance in Argentine public opinion, the idea had been that the dictatorship was solely responsible for the crisis. As the antithesis of Argentina's authoritarian past, democracy was construed not only as promising political and ethical transformation but also as guaranteeing "to feed, educate and cure," according to one of Alfonsín's campaign slogans. After hyperinflation rudely unmasked the superficiality of this diagnosis, statements by top government authorities made plain their limited concept of the way the body politic functioned socially and economically: A. Troccoli, minister of the Interior, urged one and all "to pray every morning that soaring prices remain within reasonable limits." J.C. Pugliese, economy minister at the time, said, "I don't know why the dollar keeps going up and I don't know how to make it come down." A closer look at how the inflationary metaphor worked is illustrative: although the dollar remained relatively stable, it was the Argentine currency that depreciated. But, consciously or not, the reference to the rise of the dollar pointed to an extra-Argentine relationship: the country was powerless to structurally affect a single variable, the dollar, which by definition lay outside the province of the national government.

In this context two metaphors firmly rooted in Argentine social imagery reappear in the form of two complementary disjunctions. One is between the Argentines of yesteryear who built the country and the present-day Argentines who let it fall into ruin. The second is the idea of Argentina versus the Argentines, expressed by two crossed oppositions. One is the tension between the state (Argentina) and society (Argentines), resulting from people's increasing hostility toward the former's ineptitude and degradation. Another is the tension existing between individuals (Argentines) and community (Argentina); in this view individual interests seeking egotistically to maximize benefits hurt the nation. Thus, in the same metaphor the nation is victim both of the Argentine state and of the Argentines that make it up. With imagery like this, in which victims and victimizers switch rapidly back and forth, the new collective identity was paradoxical. It was based on the dissolution of the social bond.

Historical examples from other countries indicated the urgent need to make sense of the threat of social dissolution that affects people suffering from hyperinflation. In the face of its destructive power, these societies reconstructed a sense of community by pointing a finger at the "other guy" as the guilty party. In Argentina, on the contrary, the effort to comprehend the violence of hyperinflation led to the construction of a vision based on the previously mentioned paradox in which state, society, and individuals interact with the nation.

If both Argentines and Argentina are responsible for the crisis, designating a scapegoat becomes impossible.

In hindsight this image of a guilty country in which "we are all responsible" demonstrated that radical reform was legitimate because it was the only way to avoid a monetary debacle produced by a certain type of social organization. Moreover, with the social imagery of national decadence and collective responsibility as a backdrop, the weak, slow reaction to the "social cost" of the imminent neoliberal reform to be carried out by President Carlos Menem is not surprising. In this light it appears as the price that must be paid by Argentines to Argentina for the damage caused. The fear of returning to a recent past that included the dramatic experience of hyperinflation laid the foundation for a consensus on the need to sacrifice to achieve long-term stability. Menem relied on this spirit of the times for support, which as president he reinforced by stressing the need for collective "sacrifice" that his plan for stabilizing the economy, which he termed "Convertibility," entailed, along with the "guilt" that, in the end, was shared by all Argentines for the state of affairs he had inherited.

I want to express my gratitude once again to the heroic Argentine people for their strength and understanding of a sacrifice that will not have been made in vain. (Menem, Labor Day speech, May 1, 1993)

This is how you work seriously and responsibly in a country that should never have reached the calamitous state in which we received it in 1989; the government, God forbid, was not to blame, the fault is the long years of misunderstanding among Argentines. (Menem, message to the legislature, May 1, 1993)

The legitimacy of at least Menem's first term in office (1989–95) rested on economic stability. But, tinged with the spirit of national renewal, his actions went beyond that. Politically the pardon granted the military chiefs of staff and squad leaders who had been tried and jailed for illegal repression during the Alfonsín presidency stands out in this regard. The pardon closed—temporarily—a cycle that began with the guilty verdict returned at the trial of the military juntas, whose effects had already begun to be mitigated by the Due Obedience and Full Stop laws put into effect by Alfonsín himself. But a pardon supposedly based on "national reconciliation" only reinforced the image that Argentina was not a society that followed the rule of the law.

A second action, one that affected the president's own Justicialist party, was the dismantling of the principal labor organizations and the disciplining of those remaining under the Peronist umbrella (see Acuña 1995). Although the pardon was not directly linked to economic strategy, disciplining labor was, because active opposition to the privatizations and wage freeze needed to make the Convertibility Plan viable left no alternative.

THE LEGITIMACY OF NEOLIBERAL REFORM

During the 1990s social issues were redefined both symbolically and institutionally. As we described earlier, during the first democratically elected government following the military dictatorship, social issues were inseparable from the belief in the omnipotence of political democracy; during C.S. Menem's two terms in office (1989–99), the "model," meaning the Convertibility Plan, which rigidly controlled the printing of money to avoid the risk of another round of the dreaded hyperinflation, reigned supreme as the indisputable framework within which any discussion of social questions had to be carried on. The model defined which social demands were legitimate and which were not. It was as if the state had suddenly become the head of a household on a fixed income and any additional expense would threaten the precarious balance in place. This enabled the government to disqualify demands in the name of stability. By permitting social demands to be judged in monetary terms, fiscal equilibrium was the preeminent image for deciding their legitimacy. Consequently, demands were broken down into comparable and interconnected parts, which, through their effect on the economy as a whole, were connected to the destiny of the community at large. Social demands became corporative by definition and, as such, were opposed to the common good if they threatened fiscal equilibrium.

In general this approach legitimized the severe neoliberal reforms put into effect, and, in particular, their "social cost." Of course the government was not a mere spectator but rather an actor that contributed to constructing and legitimizing the neoliberal spirit of the times. In calling the 1990s a turning point in the social and institutional structure of Argentina, what is meant is that, despite the overt intention of the military dictatorship to dismantle the import-substitution model of economic growth and the intention of the Alfonsín government to repair the damage done, the basic rules of play around which the Argentine economy was organized remained unchanged between 1975 and 1989: no important public-sector enterprise was privatized and no significant changes were made in existing labor laws, and the level of public funding for social security, education, and health was not reduced to anything like the low levels to come (Beccaria 1993).

During the 1990s the role of the state in the life of Argentines across the social spectrum changed radically, in accordance with Argentina's new strategy for growth. Economic and social reform took place within the regional framework of a debate on the role of globalization. Sectors identified with economic reform, inspired by the so-called Washington Consensus, never tired of praising the benefits of globalization, which were understood to be a "modern" economy and guaranteed economic growth; the same forces never tired of accusing those not in their camp of being isolationists. Proreform forces assumed the defense of the policies of free trade, privatization, and deregulation of market and workplace. Notwithstanding its social consequences, the neoliberal economic strategy was frequently presented as the only alternative for economic growth.

Economic strategy was based on a series of policies that began to be applied in the early 1990s (see Basualdo 2003; Damill et al. 2002; Heymann & Kosacoff 2000). The main ones were monetary convertibility (the Convertibility Plan); the reduction of the fiscal deficit, by both spending less and collecting more taxes; deregulation; and extensive privatization of public-sector enterprises. Collective bargaining was abandoned in favor of decentralized salary negotiations directly connected to productivity. The main objective of these measures was to increase savings, investment, productivity, and competitiveness.

The effect of these reforms on the Argentine economy soon became apparent. In contrast to the economy of the prior decade, inflation was brought under control, domestic investment returned, and the economy began to grow at a relatively high rate (Heymann 2000). The inflation rate declined steadily from the hyperinflationary levels reached in 1989 to a very low level in 1994; this low rate continued dropping, reaching deflationary levels by the end of the decade.

Its macroeconomic profile notwithstanding, the Argentine economy showed itself highly vulnerable to external impact. This became abundantly clear in the capital flight that took place during the Mexican crisis in 1995 and the Asiatic one in 1998. In this sense financial globalization meant little control over foreign capital, which, in crisis situations, could easily abandon the country, seriously damaging the Argentine economy. The sharp recession that began in 1998 and lasted until 2003 made clear the incapacity of this economic model to generate a strategy for sustained economic growth.

As we mentioned previously, other important consequences of neoliberal reform in Argentina were increasingly high levels of foreign debt and the widespread privatizing of public-sector enterprises. The economic growth that marked the first half of the decade was based on foreign, not domestic, investment, which fell during the second half. Argentina's gross foreign debt came to represent 32.3 percent of its GNP in 1999, which severely conditioned economic policy. Paradoxically, during this same period the privatizing of state-run telecommunications, oil and energy enterprises, and the national airline, among other enterprises, brought large sums of foreign currency into the country. Between 1990 and 1999 income derived from privatization amounted to $24 million, one of the highest figures in Latin America, topped only by Brazil and Mexico, whose economies are significantly larger than Argentina's (Bayón and Saraví 2002).

PRIVATIZATION AND ECONOMIC AUSTERITY

The size of the reduction in government spending in Argentina during the past decade is worthy of note. From an average deficit of 14.5 percent of the GNP in 1981 to 1983, the shortfall dropped to only 2 percent in 1990, and in 1992 there was a budget surplus of 0.5 percent. Public-sector salaries were one of the main variables adjusted to put Argentina in the black (see Marshall 1994).

Changed working conditions accompanied the reduction of salaries in the public sector. Lozano (1994) listed these changes as executive salaries being paid in foreign currency, which led to the demise of the civil service career professional, temporary personnel replacing permanent employees, and a salary scale heavily tipped toward the upper end. Differences in salary were accompanied by differences in benefits: whereas middle- and lower-level civil service employees belonged to bankrupt public-sector health care organizations, executives with permanent positions and upper-end contractees enjoyed private health insurance that guaranteed good health care.

In our research we examined the consequences brought about by such changes in individuals and families. They frequently mentioned feelings of inferiority regarding their social role. They were in a hostile climate, stigmatized as a result of the antistate consensus in vogue at the time. This ideological aggression, coupled with the reduced salaries that were the order of the day, generated a sense of inadequacy among teachers or doctors in public hospitals, occupations highly prized in the old days in Argentina.

The scope of the privatization process in Argentina and the rapidity with which it was carried out were unprecedented (see Azpiazu 2003; 2005). According to figures from the mid-1980s, more than three hundred state monopolies existed in Argentina in the fields of energy, rail and air transport, communications, sanitation, public utilities, and arms production, whereas state-run firms held a dominant position in the financial, petrochemical, maritime transport, and steel-producing sectors (FIEL 1988). The aggressive privatization program begun in 1989 had as its immediate objective to reduce spending and improve the public-sector cash flow, thus facilitating the fulfillment of agreements signed with the International Monetary Fund. In addition, domestic and foreign debt would be reduced by inducing creditors to swap government bonds for stock in the newly privatized companies. Unemployment also increased sharply in the 1990s because of privatization.

SOCIAL REFORM IN THE 1990S

Along with proposing economic reform, international financial organizations proposed social reform in the fields of health care, education, and social security in Latin America. The rationale given was that, to be viable, the "economic model" required less state intervention, especially in the areas requiring the greatest expenditure of government funds. Strictly speaking, the problem was not a new one. Owing to Argentina's persistent fiscal shortfalls, aggravated by the foreign debt, the level of service provided by the state had deteriorated markedly, and the underfinancing of the social security system had reached crisis proportions. For their part businessmen were more open in their opposition to protective labor regulations because of the support they received in government circles. It was in this context that the notion that social policy had to change flourished.

The rationale behind the provision of social services was radically questioned in the 1990s (Cortés and Marshall 1999). Universal health care and education were labeled inefficient and unequal because they favored the middle class at the expense of lower income strata. To correct this distributive bias and decentralize social services, the social reform proposed a strategy of focusing primarily on the poorest members of society. In the workplace the objective was to dismantle legislation protecting workers to reduce labor costs and thus become more competitive in the global marketplace. The social security system was privatized with the dual objective of reducing the fiscal deficit and increasing the pool of locally available capital (Mesa-Lago 1999).

Thus, the dismantling of the state-run and financed social sector proceeded apace, and social services became tied to the business cycle with minimal or nonexistent compensatory mechanisms in times of need. In other words, instead of acting more decisively in times of economic crisis to compensate for social consequences in the society at large—termed *anticyclical behavior*—social service austerity accompanied economic adjustment. A policy of creating a broader safety net accompanied the severe budget cutting, but, not surprisingly, it was a failure. This meant that in a context of growing unemployment and increasingly precarious working conditions for people with jobs, both unemployment benefits and free access to health care tended to be made available only to very small sectors of the chronically poor, without taking into account the needs of the contingents of recently impoverished people appearing on the scene.

Economic policy allowed little margin for social policy. Far from offering benefits and anticyclical measures to maintain basic consumption at levels that would ensure equitable growth, the tendency was to consider social policy as a secondary concern whose maximum aspiration was to reduce the so-called social cost of the model. Social spending was decreased, not increased, or rather the capacity to provide social services and fulfill basic needs in areas such as education, health, housing, and welfare was reduced (Heymann 2000.)

Nevertheless, as shown by Cortés and Marshall (1999), changes were made unevenly across the social service spectrum: reforms took place in those areas considered crucial to the success of the current economic strategy. And in these high priority areas, there was less room for political and institutional factors to block or undermine the original reform strategy. For example, reforms designed to check labor costs and reduce the cost of social security to the government were viewed as more critical for the success of the liberalization strategy than were reforms in public health and education, the latter being carried out sporadically and often partially.

Social reform in the 1990s assumed the general shape of a hybrid model, reflecting the tensions between the demand for social reform, the limited funds available for it, the persistence of institutions created under the former model, and the increase in social problems requiring an immediate response. It can be said that the priority of the state in the 1990s in the area of social policy was not to meet the concrete needs of those living in poverty but rather to satisfy the institutional and corporative requirements of different actors—local and provincial governments and multilateral organizations, for example. It was necessary to maintain equilibrium and fulfill commitments in a number of areas, while at the same time not losing the political support of labor unions and provincial governors belonging to the governing party.

SOCIAL REFORM A DECADE LATER

Any evaluation of the state's role in the 1990s indicates that social issues were not one of its primary concerns. Social policy during the past decade can be characterized as fragmented and uneven. For example, in 1998 sixty social programs for combating poverty could be found scattered among different areas of the government, often having the same target group. This fragmentary approach permitting the overlapping of programs meant a less than optimal use of at least part of the resources available. It also flew in the face of the universal tendency toward an integrated approach to combating poverty. But it would be a mistake to lay the blame for the inefficient use of resources on this fragmentation and overlapping, because funding for social programs during this period of increasing need was never adequate (See Repetto 2001).

There are additional reasons for questioning the model used for social reform. One is the existence of new social problems and vulnerable populations outside the scope of the social programs in effect. Existing programs were aimed at structural poverty pockets, meaning households with a long history of unsatisfied needs, usually located in determined habitats like temporary settlements and suburban ghettos or *villas miseria*. But the magnitude of the Argentine crisis in recent decades affected populations other than the chronically poor, as we show in the next chapter. The newly impoverished came to include the middle class when their income dropped below the poverty line. Their sociodemographic and cultural profile was different from that of the structurally poor, as were their needs and habitat—they were to be found scattered around urban areas. This meant they required different kinds of programs. The same can be said for households in which breadwinners' employment was precarious. These households also fell into poverty when income dropped. Clearly the social policy in effect offered no response to these new problems, which were largely absent from any governmental discussion.

Serious doubts remain regarding the social strategy applied during this period that aimed social programs at target groups of the chronically poor: analysis has revealed that their impact on poverty was almost nil. Nobody would deny that improving the efficiency of social programs may alleviate particular situations, but without intervention in the workplace and an active policy of income redistribution, there is no hope for reducing poverty in the region (see Lo Vuolo 1999).

THE EXPERIENCES OF URUGUAY AND CHILE

Uruguay and Chile show similarities to and differences from Argentina during the 1990s. Policies for stabilizing the economy, free trade, and deregulation were put into effect in the three countries. In Uruguay social results were not unlike what happened in Argentina: increased unemployment, worsened working conditions, reduced income levels among the middle- and lower-class members. But at the institutional level, the changes in Uruguay occurred gradually. In this sense many of the measures causing large-scale dislocation in countries like Argentina were either not put into effect at all or carried out within the framework of existing regulations and controls, with results more in accordance with the general needs of Uruguayan society than was the case in Argentina. For example, the great majority of state-run services and enterprises have remained in the public sector. The one exception is social security. According to Uruguayan specialists, even though the results of the reform constitute a clear departure from the old system, it is still state run and more openly committed to distributive objectives than in other reform programs (Kaztman et al. 1999).

The case in Chile, one of the first Latin American countries to begin "modernizing," is very different. During the dictatorship of Augusto Pinochet, state intervention was discontinued in favor of a clearly defined system of market-oriented policies. During the 1980s the neoliberal and monetarist policies adopted were evident in the day-to-day operations of the Chilean state. In the 1970s a far-reaching labor reform made conditions in the workplace precarious for ordinary Chileans. The reform included measures that made it possible to be fired without cause and that also abolished the minimum wage for minors and extended the scope of temporary employment, among others. Similar measures were applied in the fields of education, where access to secondary and higher education became increasingly dependent on individual effort and was no longer a right guaranteed by the state. Access to free health care also became increasingly limited. We should note that Chile was one of the first countries in Latin America to adopt the social strategy of focusing on the minimal needs of people living in extreme poverty while carrying out a generalized reduction of the role of the state in offering social services to the population as a whole.

In general terms Latin America has been swept by a far-reaching wave of neoliberal policies applied in different ways in different countries. Economic and social reform has become associated with—we wouldn't say caused by—a certain type of economic globalization. After comparing the Chilean, Uruguayan, and Argentine experiences, the importance of the political and social foundation on which the reforms have been carried out becomes clear. In the Chilean example the feasibility of silencing protest by out and out repression was shown. Numerous measures put into effect by the Pinochet government would have been unthinkable if they had required a consensus to sustain them. On the contrary, in Uruguay the weight of the middle class and popular sectors limited the scope of the reforms, but many of their negative effects have been felt just the same.

Argentina is one of the countries in which many of the recommended reforms were most expeditiously put into effect, bringing marked social consequences in their wake, as we show in the next chapter. In this regard it resembles—or even surpasses—Chile, and it differs from Uruguay in that in Argentina there was no counterweight to mitigate the negative effects of social and economic reform. Although the majority of these measures were put into effect by demo-cratically elected governments, the influence of the military dictatorship that ruled Argentina from 1976 to 1983, along with the hyperinflation suffered in 1989 to 1990, must be taken into account as disciplinary factors that contributed to silencing the voices of protest that had been gaining force since the mid-1980s. The legitimacy enjoyed by these economic and social reform policies cannot be detached from the two great fears marking recent Argentine history: repression and the perception that social bonds were coming undone and the country was falling apart.

Three

The impact on the social structure of the processes described previously has been so great that a new type of society has been formed. To give some idea of the extent of the changes that have taken place, we focus on five specific areas. Our hope is that this approach will provide a general picture of the new Argentine society that has emerged. First we examine the fate during the 1990s of the more or less homogeneous group of the "structurally poor," who had lived below the poverty line for a long time. Next we analyze two significant transformations that occurred in the heterogeneous Argentine middle class: the appearance of a growing category of the "newly impoverished" middle-class Argentines who fell below the poverty line, and the rise up the social scale of a much smaller sector of the same middle class. We then examine the impact of the increase in unemployment on the society at large. And finally we describe a new phenomenon in Argentina: the emergence of a sector of the population on the periphery of the working world that manages to survive by combining legal and illegal activities.

CHANGES IN STRUCTURAL POVERTY

In the first study of poverty in Latin America, carried out before the military dictatorship took power in 1976, Argentina had the lowest level in the region: 5 percent in urban areas and 19 percent in rural ones. At that time, these figures contrasted sharply with the regional averages of 26 percent and 62 percent, respectively

(Altimir 1979). Data on poverty were not kept during the military dictatorship. But, as we have already touched on, the early studies carried out when democracy returned pointed to a very different reality: in 1984, 22 percent of all Argentine households lived below the poverty line, according to the Argentine National Institute of Statistics and Censuses (INDEC). Regional variations were marked. For example, the figure for the city of Buenos Aires was 7 percent, whereas 47 percent of the rural population of Formosa, one of the poorest provinces in the country, lived in poverty.

These figures refer to what in Latin America is referred to as "structural poverty": chronically poor people who, in many cases, have migrated from the countryside to urban areas where they are found crowded into the shantytowns—called *villas miseria* in Argentina, *cantegriles* in Uruguay, and *campamentos* in Chile—surrounding big cities. The structurally poor have little or no education, have many children, and survive on the fringes of the labor market. Leading indicators for identifying them are habitat and level of education, considered the most visible signs of chronic poverty.

Changes appeared in the structurally poor sector of the population early on following the return of democracy. Between 1980 and 1990 two parallel movements occurred: on one hand, structural poverty stabilized, and on the other, the total number of households living below the poverty line increased because of the fall of middle-class families below the poverty line during the economic crises of the 1980s. This period marks the beginning of poverty caused by the recent loss of income (rather than structural poverty alone). But this newly impoverished population fell through the cracks in the statistics kept on poverty; the indicators used, especially those on habitat, applied only to the structurally poor. New instruments for measuring poverty based on income had to be implemented before this process could be tracked.

Different hypotheses arose to explain why structural poverty had stabilized. Beccaria and Vinocur (1991) emphasized the importance of infrastructure improvements such as the laying of pipelines for running water, as well as the construction of public housing for low-income families. They also mentioned home improvements made by the poor out of their savings. Because structural poverty was determined by dwelling-linked indicators, any improvement in this area supposedly meant a reduction in the number of people living in poverty.

What is important to note is that, especially during the early years of the Menem presidency when hyperinflation ended and economic growth was high, fewer structurally poor Argentines led people to believe that poverty in general was declining, and the trickle-down theory was bearing fruit, bringing the benefits of economic growth to the lowermost rungs of the social ladder. Today, however, it is abundantly clear that the situation was more complex than originally thought. Apparently a certain confusion set in: although changes occurring within the traditional poverty "map" were recorded statistically, changes in the total "territory" affected by poverty were not. Our hypothesis is that the indicators for measuring structural poverty were not sensitive enough to capture alterations within the population being measured. Be that as it may, in the early 1990s Argentina was viewed once again as a country with a growing economy and a decreasing poverty rate, although the real story was quite different.

There were two tendencies in particular that belied this rosy picture of the early years of Convertibility (1991–93). In the first place, although the number of structurally poor people

Poverty, Indigence, and Unemployment, 1988–2003, Buenos Aires

Period	Homes below Poverty Line (%)	Persons Living below Poverty Line (%)	Unemployment (%)
May 1988	22.5	29.8	6.3
Oct. 1988	24.1	32.3	5.7
May 1989	19.7	25.9	7.6
Oct. 1989	38.2	47.3	7.0
May 1990	33.6	42.5	8.6
Oct. 1990	25.3	33.7	6.0
May 1991	21.9	28.9	6.3
Oct. 1991	16.2	21.5	5.3
May 1992	15.1	19.3	6.7
Oct. 1992	13.5	17.8	6.7
May 1993	13.6	17.7	10.6
Oct. 1993	13.0	16.8	9.6
May 1994	11.9	16.1	11.1
Oct. 1994	14.2	19.0	13.1
May 1995	16.3	22.2	20.2
Oct. 1995	18.2	24.8	17.4
May 1996	19.6	26.7	18.0
Oct. 1996	20.1	27.9	18.8
May 1997	18.8	26.3	17.0
Oct. 1997	19.0	26.0	14.3
May 1998	17.7	24.3	14.1
Oct. 1998	18.2	25.9	13.3
May 1999	19.1	27.1	15.6
Oct. 1999	18.9	26.7	14.4
May 2000	21.1	29.7	16.0
Oct. 2000	20.8	28.9	14.7
May 2001	23.5	32.7	17.2
Oct. 2001	25.5	35.4	19.0
May 2002	37.7	49.7	22.0
Oct. 2002	42.3	54.3	18.8
May 2003	39.4	51.7	16.4

Encuesta Permante de Hogares.

appeared to have dropped, the intensity of existing poverty was high, meaning that its impact was as strong or stronger than before. Second during these years income inequality among the poor increased because some people came to have almost no income at all. These characteristics combined to produce among the structurally poor a new subcategory of "hardcore" poor who had no chance of ever finding a job, not even the unskilled jobs they used to get during periods of economic growth. Later this subcategory became the bedrock out of which the self-organized unemployed groups called *piqueteros* grew, which we analyze in chapter 5. This intensification of poverty has also had a significant identificatory impact: a group may be considered statistically poor without necessarily identifying itself as poor. Studies show that, beyond statistical considerations, even the most marginal presence in the labor market can earn the identification of "worker" for the person involved, a term that has occupied an important place in Peronist imagery. Being excluded from the working world makes it difficult to be included in this category, thus giving rise to identificatory strategies for not being identified as poor.

The further impoverishment of the structurally poor meant that households that in the past had been able to plot strategies and a time frame for purchasing food and clothing and improving their homes could no longer do so. In a study in the early 1980s on popular sectors, the first signs of a reduced time frame and wish list appeared. In 1980 Jelín and Feijóo concluded that "while it was once possible to 'dream' of fixing up the house or moving, a cassette tape recorder or color TV now figure among the goods dreamed of as long as installment plans make them accessible" (p. 77). Ten years later studies began to detect solidarity strategies among neighbors in popular sectors for exchanging services like tutoring sessions for meals, buying products wholesale, and holding potluck suppers. Small start-up businesses, which usually failed, were another response to the growing unemployment (Prelorán 1995).

A few years later the impact of marginalization from the workplace on poor households stood out clearly: their strategies focused exclusively on the immediate objective of feeding the family on the day in question. Even though distribution programs were highly targeted at the outset, such programs ended up including all residents of neighborhoods where there were people with no income. In these areas, the programs became an important resource for food (Cravino et al. 2002).

Changes in household strategies have repercussions on family relations. What happens to the role of women in this context? Responsibility for feeding the family falls almost exclusively on women, who are viewed as "natural" food providers. Research (Jelín 1998) indicates that women spend more time acquiring food and reorganizing the family budget—searching for the lowest prices, signing up for social programs, and so on—to meet crisis demands. No evidence has been found to support the hypothesis that this added burden outside the home has brought about more democratic gender relations within its walls. On the contrary it appears to be one more example of what has been termed the "invisible adjustment," by which is meant the extra burden resulting from women's efforts to mitigate the crisis both inside and outside the home.

THE NEW POORS

Research published in the 1990s depicted an unprecedented phenomenon in Argentina: the impoverishment of a large part of the middle class (Minujin 1992; Minujin and Kessler 1995).

Few postwar societies can match the magnitude of this middle-class pauperization, which was so widespread that it has altered the social structure of the country, as well as the image of it held by Argentines. The change was not abrupt but rather the cumulative effect of a number of factors occurring in the course of the past two decades.

In broad terms middle-class impoverishment began when the income of mid-level salaried professionals fell during the military dictatorship that took power in 1976. Suffice it to say that between 1980 and 1990 the average income of salaried personnel and wage earners dropped 40 percent. This impoverishment came about as a result of a loss in earning power, not from unemployment as was the case in Western Europe. The second phase began with the rise in unemployment and job insecurity during the first half of the 1990s. The loss of earning power suffered by the middle class redrew the poverty map. As poverty spread into Argentina's fabled middle class, the image of poverty traditionally held in Latin America could no longer be sustained. The statistics are eloquent in this regard: although the working poor represented 3.2 percent of the population in 1980, by the end of the decade the corresponding figure was 26.7 percent (INDEC 2003).

What is novel about these new poors is that they constitute a hybrid stratum of persons linked, on one hand, to the middle class by long-term economic and cultural factors—they have more education and fewer children than do the structurally poor—and, on the other, to chronically poor sectors by short-term variables caused by the crisis such as unemployment and lack of health care. The decline of the middle class has not been homogeneous: income disparity has made some members "losers" and others "winners" within each occupational category. As a result the newly impoverished include professionals, government employees, small industrialists, and administrative personnel, among others.

This quantitative heterogeneity has a qualitative correlate—differences in social trajectories with regard to type of socialization, family origin, and educational and career histories—that was not readily apparent before the crisis. Before becoming impoverished these individuals had internalized different expectations, beliefs, and classification criteria and had different social contacts. Afterward this diversity of qualitative factors among the poor gave rise to heterogeneous ways of dealing with poverty.

But above and beyond this heterogeneity, falling out of the middle class profoundly changed the daily lives of the newly impoverished, calling into question the viability of any and all household practices that cost money. One of the singularities of impoverishment is what we have termed its coercive power: it becomes necessary to constantly alter habits and routines, which makes everyday living increasingly complex. Impoverishment is experienced simultaneously as personal dislocation and also as the disorganization of the world around. This dual perception makes adaptation difficult in the classic sense of adapting to a new but definite and definable context. The new poors don't doubt that everything has changed, but they know neither where they are nor what the new world they have been catapulted into (without understanding very well why or how) is like.

Different examples of this search for meaning appear in research on the newly impoverished (Minujin and Kessler 1995; Kessler 1998). People who have fallen below the poverty line must make sense out of a situation unprecedented in Argentina in either communal experience or family histories. This middle-class impoverishment is exceptional, and as such has abruptly cut off an ongoing historical-cultural success narrative. Neither family nor cultural socialization nor common everyday strategies—not even their worst nightmare—had prepared middle-class members for this one-way trip into poverty.

What we mean by "historical-cultural success narrative" can be described as a kind of "philosophy of history," a shared narrative connecting past with future in any given society. Three main themes are articulated into a systematic whole that gives meaning to everyday practices. The first is Argentina's prosperous past and social mobility, experienced by and deeply etched into the collective memory of a large part of the population. Tulio Halperín Donghi just might be right when he says that the promises made by Argentina's founding fathers were fulfilled too rapidly. This initial good luck became the matrix for the second and third themes: a firm belief in collective progress, and the rise of the Argentine middle class, respectively.

Within the framework of this historical-cultural saga, even the inexplicable—the recurrent crises suffered by a country so richly endowed—made sense. But progress came at a cost, and the pursuit of individual advancement by selfish individuals undermined nation building, which seemed abundantly clear during the 1989–90 hyperinflation crisis. But up to that point at least, the constant interplay of this zero-sum game between society and nation had resulted in relatively prosperous *Argentines,* albeit at the cost of the nation as a whole. What was not contemplated in this particular historical-cultural tale was that it would end unhappily with the demise of the Argentine middle class.

This historical-cultural model was reinforced by a generational model according to which each generation rose a rung or more above its predecessor on the social ladder. In the worst case it stayed in the same place; social descent was out of the question. The themes from the historical-cultural tale reappeared in each individual's personal story of family ups and downs. But in both cases the overriding tendency was always upward and onward to such a degree that "progress" and "future" were synonymous. Family histories varied, but a definitive fall was outside the realm of possibility. Impoverishment with no possibility of recovery has closed the book on this particular success story. And its possible sequel—the threat of ever-greater impoverishment as children fall even further—would suggest its cruel reversal.

One result of the turnabout in this historical-cultural and generational model is a situation of general unintelligibility in which nobody knows how to explain, much less typify, this new experience in terms of the stock themes provided by Argentine history.[1] Because irrevocable impoverishment was never an option, behavior models for confronting it are nonexistent. Such was not the case during the hyperinflation period, because inflation is something that has figured prominently in modern Argentine history (see Botana and Waldmann 1988; Sigal and Kessler 1997).

This cultural breakdown has also weakened the ideological nucleus at the heart of Argentines' view of themselves and their country. In a society characterized by economic, political, and social instability, the mythical tale of collective progress functioned as a kind of collective glue: a series of generally agreed upon, stable principles that, until now, seemed to hold things together no matter what. It goes without saying that without the inevitability of progress, this ideological nucleus falls apart. The only possible replacement in sight to date—the belief in stability as a common will—is not the same at all.

Be that as it may, the newly impoverished can be thought of as a metaphor for globalization in Argentina. Not only are they a consequence of this transformation but also, above all, the difficulty impoverished middle-class members have in understanding what happened to them is analogous to Argentines' conflicting views on the place of Argentina in the world at large. In hindsight other unpleasant surprises during the past thirty-two years laid the groundwork for this one. The most recent one was the 2001 default crisis when, believing themselves on the doorstep of the first world, they found themselves, terrified, entering the third: from being the poster child of international organizations, Argentina became close to anathema in the eyes of the rest of the world. Another was the allegedly unknown—or willfully ignored—dimensions of state terrorism during the last military dictatorship. And yet another was the 1982 Falklands War, at the beginning of which Argentines fantasized that the United States would take their side, and later on that they were winning when the war was already lost. Although there is no reason why a country's social imagery must necessarily coincide with what is later defined as "reality," there is little question that the negative qualities of the periodic crises suffered by Argentina have been exacerbated by the maladjustment between expectation and reality embodied in the Argentine middle class's view of itself.

SOCIAL IDENTITY UNDER FIRE

The trouble the newly impoverished have in categorizing themselves socially makes evident this extreme discomfort with self-identification. Specifically, do they say they belong to the "middle class" or are they "poor"? Self-classification involves situating oneself imaginatively within a given social structure in accordance with one's position in the social world. For example, a middle-class category presupposes the existence of a lower class and an upper class; thus, changing how one categorizes oneself can mean a different view of the social order as a whole.

The question now is how impoverishment affects previously held identification schemes. Assuming the lack of an a priori reason for changing categories, except for the unemployed, there is nothing to oblige one to change categories. Without a "destitution rite"—as in the case of an administrative employee who, after losing his job, becomes an unemployed professional—there is no overriding reason for change. But, as we observed previously, impoverishment does call into question membership in the middle class, which has been historically linked to the problematical definition of what it means to be Argentine. In surveys conducted in the 1980s, more than 70 percent of the population said they belonged to the middle class, the magnitude of the figure being precisely what differentiated Argentina from the rest of Latin America in the past.

During hyperinflation, references to the "decline and fall of the middle class" raised the specter of the annihilation of a social stratum and the nation-building project that it embodied. Its disappearance would turn the tripartite equilibrium that characterized Argentina up to that point into an upper- and lower-class confrontation. Argentina would then look like Brazil, which, in Argentine social imagery, has been an example of a dual society suffering from poverty and violence. Hyperinflation was a devastating phenomenon that was felt in every corner of Argentine public life. By affecting all social sectors in some way, hyperinflation did a lot to turn doubts about the viability of individual membership in the Argentine middle class into a question of whether the social class would survive at all.

But as impoverishment occurs over time, it is less visible as a social problem than chronic poverty, which makes it more likely to be formulated in individual terms. This makes the question of whether they still belong to the middle class a critical one for the newly impoverished, who have attempted to answer it in a number of ways. It is not surprising that an across-the-board weakening of middle-class social identity that has taken place has led to a questioning of the generally accepted criteria for membership, such as the importance of social position in the past and that of educational and cultural levels. The extent of impoverishment is also controversial: Does it affect only a single social sector or the society at large? And finally, if the newly impoverished are no longer members of the middle class, what social class do they belong to?

For the newly impoverished, at bottom, the identity question is simple: the middle class still exists, and either one belongs to it or one doesn't. Some people say they still belong because they possess attributes that compensate for the loss of earning power, such as diplomas, job category, cultural level, customs, the past, and so on. Others make reference to "*the massive devaluation of the middle class*," for all of those whose living conditions have declined. Nevertheless, they go on to say, the middle class and its members are alive, though not necessarily well. Similar views are heard from people who think the middle class has been altered qualitatively enough to merit a new classification: "upper lower class," for example. Here the change is viewed as collective. The same tripartite social structure persists, only now the segment separating upper and lower classes has a new name. Granted its social position is not what it used to be; it is now closer to the lower class as illustrated by the testimonies that follow, which date from the mid-1990s:

> *There's no money, there's simply no money. There's no over-time, there's nothing. You have to invest your money well, don't you? What I mean is that you can't buy a pair of shoes if you don't know if you can make it to the end of the month. Before you could count on overtime to pay for a whole lot of things. But there's no overtime anymore. That's the problem. Things have gone downhill a lot. There's no middle class anymore, in other words, we're a high lower class.*

> *It's going to be like in Brazil or Chile with an upper class and a lower class. The upper class is going to be with the people on top, the opportunists, and those people are going to do fine. But everybody else is going to have a very hard time. And they won't have any right to complain. There's no unions anymore or anybody else to defend them. We're going to go back to the times of slavery. You'll get paid a pittance, and if you like it, fine, and if you don't, that's fine too. But those who are really bad off are the ones who have always had a bad time. They've sunk to the bottom of the ocean now. And we're in their place, trying not to sink any farther.*

Maintaining middle-class membership requires not only trying to maintain certain practices but also avoiding others that, if adopted, would confirm that expulsion has taken place. In relative, hierarchical terms, staying in a certain social category implies remaining on the right side of certain limits imposed by the definition itself. This explains the attitude of many of the people interviewed that they had no right to accept welfare and food handouts from the government. As the poor are the rightful recipients of these social benefits, to receive either would mean one was poor. Welfare benefits label the recipient; by refusing the benefit, the stigma is avoided.

The alternative was to consider oneself expelled. In those cases "lifestyle" was the crux of belonging. Self-expulsion was more frequent among people without university degrees or those who occupied nonprofessional positions; in other words, they lacked the attributes necessary to compensate for deteriorating living conditions. There was no clear-cut dividing line, however. People in objectively similar situations opted for one or the other position according to whether they viewed the glass as half empty or half full—"*after all, I'm still a professional*"—was emphasized in the latter case. Expulsion from the middle class might trigger a search for another social category to belong to, but in no case did these people consider themselves poor. Poverty was structural, which meant it was ruled out by both their past lifestyle and their present lifestyle. They attempted instead to find some category that would take into account the heterogeneity of their experience, as illustrated in the following testimony:

Middle class was the class that had some kind of educational preparation, it was the one where people could go to secondary school, where they could aspire to something better, I'm speaking of how it was in my day, right? I'm 40 years old. Middle class were those people whose children had some kind of higher education because in those days only primary education was the rule. But now this is debatable. I'd call it working class. I really don't know if I'm middle class or lower

*class. I know I'm working class because we depend on wages
that we have to work hard to get, but economically you could
say we are poor class, our income is pretty low, my husband
is the breadwinner, so things get more and more difficult.
Now if you take into the account the place you live, the kind
of house you have, ours isn't a shack, we have running water,
gas, some education, so we could be middle class. But I no
longer know where I belong: I'm middle class or I'm poor
class according to the circumstances.*

This testimony shows that, just as we do, the woman interviewed considers the newly impoverished to be a hybrid stratum, with consumption patterns, social relations, property, needs, and traditional beliefs assignable to different social groups. This hybridity makes it possible for people to answer questions on middle-class identity in a variety of ways. In the last example the woman, unable to decide between middle and poor class, opts for working class, which implies a different set of classification guidelines extending from lifestyle to source of income (wage earner). Rather than definitive answers, however, doubts are expressed, and the social category the family belongs to is left in suspense. In some cases "identity drift" became so strong that the interviewee asked the authors, as social scientists, to define the new situation.

*No, not middle class any longer, I wish I were! There are the
poor, who have always been poor with no chance of escaping
poverty. Maybe. God forbid I ever become poor, I certainly hope
not. The poor are below where I am ... I don't know. I know that
I'm not in the middle class, but luckily I'm not poor either. ...
And you, as sociologist, where would you put me?*

Moreover, identifying oneself as belonging to the middle class was closely associated with how Argentina is viewed, both within the country and without. Argentina, like belonging to the middle class, has been historically defined in terms of what differentiates it from other Latin American countries. The stereotype of the latter is that of societies with a small elite at the top of the social pyramid, a multitude of poverty-stricken people at the bottom, with a gulf of conflict and violence in between. Thus, when the "Latin Americanization of Argentina" was spoken of in the 1990s, this is the image the speaker had in mind. In other words, the loss of its middle class would mean the disappearance of the characteristic most identified with what makes the country Argentina and its inhabitants Argentines.

Transformations in the New Poors

As happened with the structurally poor, transformation within the ranks of the newly impoverished occurred during the 1990s. Unlike what happened in Western Europe, until the mid-1990s, the chief cause of impoverishment in Argentina was the loss of earning power, not unemployment.

With the sharp rise in unemployment from 1995 on, the situation changed. From then on the newly impoverished included both working poor and unemployed. But although mass unemployment in Argentina, because of its novelty, caught the eye of researchers, who then set out to study it, the impact of this phenomenon on the society as a whole, especially on the structurally poor, has been largely ignored. The loss of earning power and jobs in the public sector, as well as in small businesses and industrial firms in the private sector during the early 1990s, set the stage for displaced members of the impoverished middle class to replace the structurally poor in the unskilled jobs the latter had traditionally held during times of economic growth. Furthermore, the new low-paid jobs opened up by technology in this same period demanded skills that the chronically poor did not have. So within the ranks of the structurally poor came a pool of older unskilled workers with no place at all now in the job market. With the formation of a hard-core sector among the traditional poor, one result of middle-class impoverishment was the restructuring of the class below into the poor and the even poorer.

After more than a decade of impoverishment, the population categorized as newly impoverished has also been transformed. In the first place, social problems such as the embargoing of dwellings and other property due to an accumulated debt load have occured with increasing frequency. And, second, many "work alternatives," viewed in the past as exclusively indicating downward mobility, are now termed *unstable trajectories*. This is because during the period of economic growth in the early 1990s, people's lots improved, only to decline again during the next economic downturn.

Further complicating matters is a factor brought about by two coexisting phenomena. One is the upward mobility that accompanied the modernization of the economy in the 1990s: more jobs requiring skills considered middle class were created. But the jobs were low paid and unstable, so the benefits and well-being derived from them were not as good as such jobs in the previous era. Consequently an individual could be upwardly mobile (intra- or intergenerationally) in the sense that his present job required a higher level of skills than past jobs he or his family had held, but he earned less money. This process we have termed *spurious mobility* (Kessler and Espinoza 2003).

Transformations occurring in the 1990s also altered the traditional guidelines for upward mobility and social stratification. Called *contingent mobility,* it occurs when upward mobility according to objective criteria is perceived as downward in direction by the person holding the job because it is unstable. As a result of increasing job contingency, a lower-ranking but secure job becomes more desirable. When all is said and done, advancement careerwise and even salarywise does not necessarily increase well-being if the future is uncertain. The issue of contingent mobility calls into question the categories used for measuring social mobility in both Argentina and the Southern Cone. Are they in accord with the significance individuals attach to their job history, or is there instead a gap between the objective categories used for measurement and the subject's personal perception?

The newly impoverished sector's relationship to politics and collective action has also been transformed. In the early 1990s poverty was something to be ashamed of and hidden, so no group action or collective strategies were initiated. Later on, as we show in chapter 5, undertakings such as barter clubs—an arrangement for exchanging goods and services that involved around two million people at its peak—appeared. Then, following the events of December 2001, the impoverished middle class, no longer ashamed, took to the streets, forming neighborhood assemblies and pressure groups made up of people whose savings had been frozen and then devalued by the banks.

Categories of social identity have also transformed. The resistance to being considered poor and feelings of "identification drift" we described previously are much less prominent at the present time than in the mid-1990s when the research was done. Many people now have no problem describing themselves in sociological terms as "newly impoverished." Recent studies also indicate a change in the cause given for this decline in fortune. In the past, people tended to blame themselves for their social decline. But, thanks to the prominent place globalization and the effects of neoliberal reform now occupy in public opinion, the recently impoverished can now view their personal history in a historical context and see their destiny as a collective one.

At this point in time, the ranks of the decade-old "newly" impoverished are heterogeneous. New groups with different characteristics and trajectories appear and disappear. The situation is becoming increasingly fluid and complex as structural macrosocial processes affect living conditions, the meaning given to the experience of poverty, and the newly impoverished's relationship with other social strata.

THE RISING MIDDLE CLASS

The dramatic nature of middle-class impoverishment in Argentina should not conceal the fact that part of the middle class managed to "stay put"; that is, their situation remaining essentially unchanged, while a small minority climbed higher on the social ladder. There is no better indicator than the increasingly unequal distribution of income during the 1990s to make this point: the decade opened with the average income of the richest 10 percent of all households in Argentina receiving around 20 times more than the average income of the lowest 10 percent; by the end of the decade the corresponding figure for the richest households had climbed to 30 times more (Altimir and Beccaria 1999). Along with the traditional upper class, the "winners" include middle-class sectors employed in the most dynamic sectors of the economy. Svampa (2002) studied this stratum; her point of departure was their flight to the suburbs during the 1990s, during which time more than 400 private communities and country clubs were built on the outskirts of Buenos Aires and other large Argentine cities such as Córdoba, Rosario, and Mendoza.

This suburbanizing wave has affected Argentina's urban physiognomy. The essentially European model of "open cities" has given way to a regime of "closed suburbs" along North American lines. The former is centered around the notion of public spaces and values such as political citizenship and social integration; the latter, on the other hand, places emphasis on private citizenship and reinforces social fragmentation. Argentina maintained the open city for many years, which rested on the foundation of the commonly held belief in the desirability of a democratic society. Within such a context, social integration can be characterized as a process that articulates horizontal relationships within social groups and vertical bonds with other sectors of the social pyramid. An open city also provides several public spaces—public schools, parks, neighborhood corners—where this process can take place.

The flight to formerly upper-class suburbs by middle-class winners has reduced their links to their less successful counterparts. This will undoubtedly further dilute what remains of the cultural homogeneity of the traditional Argentine middle class because, in the new private communities, successful middle-class members rub elbows with members of the traditional upper class. Svampa observed that, despite differences in economic and social capital and in seniority, the two groups share experiences based on common consumption patterns and tastes in home design. In some cases shared areas include the workplace. In a word the private communities have become a cultural and social framework where a new set of relationships are laying the foundation for new forms of sociability. Once the breakup of the old middle class is consummated and a small segment becomes ensconced higher up on the social ladder, the stage is set for what the researcher calls "upward integration." This she defines as the day-to-day discovery on the part of winners that, above and beyond status incongruity, they share more than they thought with their social superiors.

NEW POVERTY IN THE SOUTHERN CONE

Little research has been conducted on Latin American middle classes, in part because of the shadow cast by the image of dual societies. According to recent studies, however, middle classes have doubled in Latin American countries during the past decade (Portes and Hoffman 2003). Other Southern Cone middle classes have points in common with each other and share differences with the destiny of the Argentine middle class. The Chilean middle class experienced impoverishment early on as a result of the public-sector reforms carried out by General Pinochet (1973–88). Lomnitz and Melnick (1991) described the preceding "buddy" (*compadrazgo*) system in which favors were exchanged informally within the middle class—a job recommendation, a place in a good school, the speeding up of paperwork—that took place primarily among civil servants. The study describes the crisis that occurred when the public sector was reformed: with the middle class no longer dominating public institutions, the buddy system fell apart.

Impoverishment has once again become a concern in Chile, almost two decades later, but from a totally different perspective. For a time the "emerging Chilean middle class" created by the upward mobility of a new social group linked to the expanding service sector was frequently commented on (Ugalde and Prieto 2001). Since then, the limitations of the economic model in force and the bottoming out of the decades-long descent into poverty of large numbers of people have brought the issue of the "new poverty" to the fore.[2] Although an increase in job opportunities and higher wages reduced poverty significantly for a time, inequality is still sharply evident. That low-income sectors suffer the most when jobs are lost or wages reduced proves this point.

The increase in unemployment beginning in 1998 has tended to aggravate the vulnerability of the poor. In a system with high structural unemployment and a job market that favors skilled workers, a new phenomenon has appeared: the hard-core poor, people, and households that lack the resources and minimal opportunity required to find a place in the job market. In this sense "new poverty" in present-day Chile is linked to the relative leveling off of the levels of indigence, not to the impoverishment of sectors of the middle class as is the case in Argentina. On the other hand, although poverty has diminished notably in the past two decades, inequality has remained stable. In fact figures from the Gini index of inequality indicate that poverty has been "uncoupled" from inequality: a decrease in the former will not necessarily affect the latter. Moreover, the Gini indicator for Chile averaged 0.538 during the 1990s (Larrañaga 1999); in Argentina, on the other hand, with a higher percentage of people living in poverty and a lower rate of economic growth, although the Gini indicator did increase from 0.453 in 1990 to 0.490 in 1998 (Repetto 2001), it is still significantly lower than in Chile.

The case of Uruguay is different.[3] The Uruguayan society has been characterized by a strong tradition of social justice and democracy and little tolerance for high levels of inequality. The changes occurring during the 1990s were partly attenuated by this political-cultural feature. There is no denying, however, that fissures have appeared in Uruguayan social solidarity. This is especially true as cities become increasingly segmented along economic lines into upper-class and lower-class neighborhoods (Kaztman 2003). As public spaces for the mingling of different social strata disappear, it becomes more and more difficult for socializing not based on economic status to take place.

UNEMPLOYMENT AND ITS EFFECTS

The transformations begun in the 1970s signaled the end of full employment policies in Argentina. Clearing the way for unrestricted foreign trade in the context of an economic recession cannot help but seriously affect job opportunities. This process expelled a large number of people from the formal economy, thus increasing the number of informal jobs and worker vulnerability. These signs of change were visible to a greater or lesser degree in the 1980s, but it wasn't until the next decade that it became evident that the Argentine job market had changed.

Around 1994, at the height of the successful phase of Convertibility, Argentine society discovered that economic growth did not necessarily imply more jobs. The reconversion of the productive apparatus and the growing protagonism of the financial and service sectors of the economy opened a breach between an increase in the GNP and job creation. In point of fact, the number of jobs did grow slightly at first, but most of the new jobs were short term or part-time, and growth soon halted. Then began the emergence of the two phenomena that came to characterize the decade as a whole: contingent jobs and unemployment.

In 1995 Argentine society received a blow to the illusions raised by the Convertibility Plan: unemployment reached 18 percent, in large part due to the so-called tequila effect of the Mexican crisis. Argentine vulnerability to the whims of foreign capital was clear. Toward the end of the year, the economy began to recover, and between 1996 and 1998 unemployment dropped to slightly above 5 percent. But, we should note, neither job quality nor salaries improved at all. In mid-1998 the country began to sink into recession once again (accompanied by a drop in foreign investment). Unemployment then began to rise and didn't stop until 2003.

Above and beyond the chilling figures that depict Argentine workers' traumatic experience in the 1990s, several qualitative changes in the job market took place during this time. To begin with, the role of a job at the heart of social life was weakened, and although unemployment grew, so did job contingency, underemployment, and work done off the books. Manufacturing jobs also disappeared, as did traditional civil service jobs, and the service sector grew. The new job picture is vastly different from the old one: large sectors of the population are either unemployed or holding contingent jobs; there are new, increasingly complex requirements for getting a job, as well as a generally devastating forecast for many areas of the job market. In general, job contingency and unemployment have affected the working class in particular and Argentine society as a whole. The bargaining power of workers, much less organized than in the past, has been greatly diminished, whereas management, in turn, is much stronger than before. A weakening of labor legislation so as to flexibilize the workplace and reduce benefits further confirms this situation (see Altimir & Beccaria 1999; Rofman 1997).

Changes in the working world cannot be dissociated from economic integration into the world market in Latin American countries, whose capacity to introduce autonomous economic (monetary and fiscal) policies affecting employment and salaries has been significantly reduced. The supporters of globalization have stated that job creation can be sustainable only in a competitive context allowing for productivity increases and reduced production costs. Labor reform was recommended to increase access to the job market, the underlying assumption being that regulation costs discouraged employment creation and that deregulation would allow the free operation of the labor market. Labor reform would enable flexible hiring and ease the ability to dismiss workers and limit wage indexing and collective-bargaining agreements that drove up income levels. Recommendations included the reform of regulations affecting indirect labor costs such as employer and employee contributions to social security, as well as a reduction in unemployment compensation. It was expected that after such reforms competitiveness, productivity, and employment levels would increase.

Labor reform took place in the majority of the region, but Argentina and Peru underwent more comprehensive reform than the other countries. Reforms in Brazil, Colombia, and Panama changed, albeit to a lesser degree, core elements in labor relationships, and very few changes were made in Chile, Ecuador, Guatemala, and Nicaragua. The International Labour Office (Vega Ruíz 2001) concludes that reform has been radical in eleven out of seventeen countries, encompassing 70 percent of the region's wage earners.

Globalization is associated with the transformation of hiring conditions and wage structures, both of which affect wage earners' rights. Permanent employment has been replaced by contingent jobs, with no access to social security, and irregular income. The evasion of employer contributions to social security has greatly reduced the protection of the working population and its families when faced with several risks—illness and retirement, among others. Moreover, inequalities in the access to stable, protected jobs have further widened the gap between formal and informal—poor—workers.

The worldwide literature concerning the relationship between globalization and equity in the labor market points out the changes in the employment relationship: flexibility in hiring and dismissal regulations, irregular employment, and the loss of many of the advantages of regular, protected forms of employment. Moreover, it has been argued that labor reform preceded the extension of social vulnerability because not only the poor but also the falling middle classes have suffered the consequences of labor market deregulation. In sum, labor reform did not solve the employment problem. Rather, during the 1990s, growing unemployment, income inequalities, and insecurity expanded in the region.

YOUNG PEOPLE ON THE BORDERLINE

Within the framework of an unstable job market, there is a segment of the population, made up primarily of young people, that subsists by combining legal and illegal activities. Their situation is the direct result of the way the working world and social security protection have been transformed. Thus, unemployment is linked to another issue that, along with the economic situation, is of grave concern to people in Argentina and around the world: urban insecurity.

Given Latin America's notoriously high crime rate, the preoccupation with security runs particularly deep in the region. In Argentina crime in general—and theft in particular—rose in the 1990s. In many cases the persons involved had worked before or were working at the time the crime was committed. This undercuts the traditionally held belief that the worlds of work and crime are mutually exclusive.

Concretely the relationship between crime and unemployment continues to be controversial in developed countries. In spite of the link made between the two within public opinion, existing research neither confirms nor denies the assumption that unemployment leads to crime; results differ according to the variables—region, period, country, among others—used (see Freeman 1983). Aggregate data assumed some *correlation* between increases in crime and unemployment for decades. But after exhaustively reviewing existing empirical data in the late 1980s, Chiricos (1987) demonstrated that any positive correlation was questionable. Results also have been mixed in Argentina. Although Kusznir (1997) and Navarro (1997) found a correlation between unemployment and crime, other researchers, such as Pompei (1999), gave more credence to the increase in unequal income distribution. Thus, according to the latter, a 10 percent increase in income inequality would increase the crime rate by 3 percent.

The economic interpretation of crime customarily suffers from two fallacies. In general there exists the risk of an ecological fallacy or the extrapolating of valid relationships from the macrolevel and using them to explain individual acts. Specifically this would mean assuming that, in any given period of rising crime and unemployment rates, the unemployed commit the crimes. Another fallacy for Argentine researchers is not distinguishing the characteristics of unemployment in Argentina from those of unemployment in other countries. Actually the greatest problem in the Argentine job market isn't long-term unemployment[4] as is the case in Europe; it is chronic job instability, whose consequences can be differentiated from those of unemployment or poverty.[5]

First of all, what do we mean by job instability? Altimir and Beccaria (1999) pointed out that the majority of the jobs created in the 1990s were low-paying contingent ones with neither benefits nor severance pay. Thus, volatility was high, implying very unstable income levels. Persons with less education and skills, especially young people just entering the job market, fill jobs such as these. Indeed, a growing number of employment histories show people moving from one contingent job to another, with periods of unemployment and underemployment in between, as well as periods of absence from the job market when the person gives up looking for work.

A study carried out on a group of young people with contingent jobs showed that the majority of its members had held jobs either before or during the time in which they engaged in illegal activities (Kessler 2004). Hence, these were not full-time criminals but rather people who combined—simultaneously or successively—legal and illegal activities. In fact this was not a totally new problem; in many cases respondents' fathers, who had entered the job market in the 1980s, had unstable job histories too. This explains the difficulty some respondents had when asked the traditionally simple question "*What does your father do?*" The formerly common answer "*He's a worker or salesman*" was seldom heard. Instead, after some hesitation, they described what their father was or had been doing recently: "*I believe he delivers some kind of boxes.*"

As the image of a stable job disappears from the experience transmitted by fathers or other adults to their children, labor instability is naturalized. Young people come to see nothing more than the prospect of a long line of contingent jobs that offer no hope for progress or advancement. Not attempting to hide his bitterness, one respondent said: "*What do I have to hope for? Best case, a crappy job that pays $180 for three months. Then nothing for a while. Then another crappy job for $180 or $200 for a while. Then nothing again ... and that's how it's always going to be.*" These young people imagined— best case—a series of contingent jobs demanding few skills and paying little, interrupted by periods of unemployment.

When job instability has made it difficult to imagine any progress whatsoever in the future, a job in the present is seen as just one way of getting some money. Other ways include asking for money on the street, "putting the squeeze on,"[6] "paying toll,"[7] and robbery; the means of getting money depending on the right opportunity and the right moment. Some of the young people we interviewed combined different kinds of work with robbery, and some alternated contingent jobs with petty crime when unemployed. Others had a main activity—in some cases, robbery; in others, a job—and an odd job as sources of income. In some cases the young men and their fellow workers stole on the weekend.

When work is combined with robbery, a "two-money" regime is established: the hard-earned money made working is used for basic expenses such as helping out at home and transporting to and from work; the "other money," obtained more easily through petty crime, is spent on dates, beer, brand-name sneakers, or gifts. Fernando, a young man who lives in greater Buenos Aires, told us that at first, on weekdays, he did chores for family members and neighbors, who paid him a little; on weekends he stole with a more or less fixed group.

I did something with my uncle; I gave him a hand, painting things, cutting the grass for my other uncle, things like that, I always had money. I got by until the weekend on that, and then, then I had the other money.

The dual-occupation systems can last for years:

"I worked for a while in a bakery afterwards, there I got used to working, mostly as a baker. I was with older people, people who went around doing very well stealing, and sometimes I stole with them and earned very good money, very good money."

What did you do during that time?

"Both things, stealing and working. I did odd jobs, but it was better to steal than do odd jobs, odd jobs didn't pay, with stealing you had more money."

Did you do both things at the same time?

"Yes, even steven. Six years. Let's say six months good and six months bad. Six months straight and six months crooked."

How should going from one job to combining a job with other activities, which we have termed "the passage from the rationale of a worker to that of a supplier," be thought of? The difference is to be found in the source of legitimacy of the resources obtained. According to the worker's rationale, legitimacy resides in the *origin* of the money, which is the fruit of honest labor in a respectable, socially recognized occupation. Simple as it seems when put into words, this rationale is one of the pillars on which popular culture has been built. This honest, socially recognized labor was the collective matrix for the image of a respectable family whose breadwinner occupied a legitimate place among the adults living in popular neighborhoods.

According to the rationale of the supplier, however, legitimacy resides not in the origin of money but in its being used to satisfy needs. In other words, irrespective of origin, any resource that satisfies needs is legitimate. The latter are not limited to so-called basic needs such as food and shelter; they can also include others defined by the individuals, such as helping out their mother or paying a utility bill. Others cannot be ruled out: buying clothes, beer, or marijuana; celebrating a friend's birthday; or even going to see the Iguazú waterfalls.

The criteria for the legitimacy of what is supplied are as follows: any act that supplies resources to satisfy needs is legitimate, regardless of whether it is legal. Moreover, legitimacy and legality become uncoupled to the degree that an illegal act that satisfies a need is more legitimate than an legal one that does not. The following story illustrates this point: Omar lived with his mother and two older brothers. One of them worked in a sawmill, the other worked in construction, and Omar committed armed robberies in supermarkets. Omar spent a long time criticizing his brothers during his interview: "*They have a free ride. My mother works, she's going to be sixty years old and she works. So I started robbing, facing the music, to bring home money to pay the bills, for food, utilities, city taxes … while they spend their money on themselves.*"

The first question posed here is if Omar and the interviewees like him no longer differentiate between working and stealing. Although we don't feel in a position to affirm this is the case, what is clear is the exclusively instrumental attitude toward work. It no longer occupies the key position as basis for the construction of individual identity and peer relationships. In the case of the young men interviewed, the jobs they were able to get do not form the basis of any kind of subjective experience, whether it be the desire for full social integration and upward mobility or the different forms of resistance to exploitation that have arisen in the course of the history of popular sectors.

Paradoxically, the fading of the borderline between work and crime also has contributed to the fact that these young men are not oriented toward a career in crime either, as professional criminals in the old days were. What brought about the deprofessionalization of illegal activity? An initial observation is that the crisis in the old-fashioned criminal career coincides with that of legal occupations. From this perspective, in research into "careers gone astray" by Becker (1963), written when jobs were stable, an isomorphism between the two types of careers appears: the criminal career offered a clear horizon when legal work did. Despite their opposition, they shared the symmetry of similar rules of play. Regarding the case in question, in an era characterized by the hegemony of stable, full-time work, the idea of career as a predetermined trajectory excluding other options was perfectly feasible. When the perspective of having a career job disappears, however, the possibility of articulating different ways of obtaining resources becomes an option.

Nevertheless, the problem of job instability is not limited to income. A close examination of job experiences show that unstable jobs can never be expected to generate the type of socialization traditionally associated with work. These young men have experienced the kind of contradiction well described by Sennett (2000) in other social sectors as characteristic of late (1998?) capitalism: experiences are ephemeral, changing; there is a lack of clear rules of play; and principles of loyalty and confidence are slow to develop and sink roots in institutional cracks. Short passages describe diverse occupations that can't be attributed to any particular trade or activity. On one hand, the instability frustrates the generation from obtaining any sort of working identity, such as belonging to a particular trade, union, or firm. And on the other hand, the formative role of the workplace has been losing ground for persons excluded from secondary or tertiary education. It's not simply a question of dropping out of school, because many young people in other generations didn't go to secondary school either. Rather, on-the-job training is impractical for jobs without minimal stability. Bonds with fellow workers are also difficult when jobs are short term; when there is no job security, lasting bonds within work groups are unlikely to form. All the training and socializing formerly associated with the workplace are limited by the quantity and quality of jobs held. Lacking its traditional attributes, work becomes strictly instrumental and, as such, more closely resembles a source of supply.

In sum, heterogeneous sectors within the ranks of the poor, the rise of certain middle-class sectors and new forms of spatial segregation, unemployment, job contingency, and new sectors of the population that alternate legal activities with petty crime are all manifestations of the profound social changes occurring in Argentine society in recent decades. These are some of the consequences. But these changes have not been suffered passively. In chapter 5 we examine how people have organized and what new forms of collective action they have generated.

New Xenophobias, New Ethnic Politics
Four

During the 1990s the Argentine government and mass media announced on different occasions the arrival in Argentina of a new wave of immigrants, comparable to the transatlantic migration of the late nineteenth and early twentieth centuries. This time around, however, the immigrants were from the border countries of Bolivia, Paraguay, and Peru. The Argentine government took this to mean that Argentina had entered the first world: Germany had Turkish immigrants, the United States had Mexicans, and Argentina had Bolivians. But at the same time, according to government officials, the growing unemployment and lack of security announced at that time were also a result of immigration: the exorbitant number of border immigrants were taking jobs from Argentines and were also responsible for the high crime rate.

Sociodemographic figures, however, showed no qualitative jump in the number of border immigrants entering Argentina, nor did the figures support the claim that immigration was behind the growing unemployment and crime rates. Therefore, what needs to be explained is why large sectors of the population believed the official version. We argue in the present chapter that migration served to condense contradictions in the regional integration project examined earlier while at the same time highlighting deeper contradictions at work in Argentine society.

Let us state at the outset that although this xenophobia clearly arose out of the need to find a scapegoat for the ongoing economic and social crisis, this is, at best, a half-truth, the other half of which we cover later. Along with all the other changes occurring in Argentina in the 1990s, ethnic diversity came to be "hypervisualized." This tendency to ethnicize formerly invisible differences was a response on the part of Argentines to the ever-greater organizing activity of border migrants at the time. They were organizing both to gain legal status in Argentina and to counter the negative value attached to their identity with rhetoric of "cultural diffusion." This fetishization of differences should be viewed as part of a global shift in which multicultural politics and the demand for recognition became the order of the day. Several Latin American countries incorporated multiculturalism into their constitution, legal system, and politics during the 1990s. International organizations also were also working to strengthen groups traditionally excluded from the social mainstream, making funding available to them as well.

This global process acquired a dynamic of its own in Argentina, considered by many Argentines—and Latin Americans as well—to be a "European enclave" with no blacks or Indians. This is, of course, another half-truth: although a large number of Argentines did "descend from ships" (both physically and metaphorically) in the nineteenth and early twentieth centuries, in fact a significant part of the population was not Argentine in this sense at all. Rather, it was essentially the same sort of population that dominates the makeup of other Latin American nations. Ethnically invisible in Argentina, its specific ancestry had essentially been expunged when it was socially and politically incorporated into the import substitution economic model and Peronism.[1]

"Border immigrants," who have made up around 2.5 percent of the Argentine population since the nineteenth century, were also invisible until the 1990s. Especially in the case of Paraguayans and Bolivians, they were perceived of and placed en masse in the same category as the invisible *mestizo* Argentines: *cabecitas negras* or "little black heads." This term had been used derogatorily since the 1930s to stigmatize, in "a country without blacks," the working-class population of Indian ancestry that came from the provinces to work in Buenos Aires factories. In other words, any differentiation based on national origin or ethnic specificity tended to be dissolved into a racially tinged social class identification that covered both Argentine *mestizos* and border immigrants. The poor were "black," even though they had no African blood and looked nothing like a "black" according to classification systems as different from each other as those of Brazil and the United States.

THE ARGENTINE NARRATIVE AND ETHNIC DEMARKATION

According to the myth, Argentina is a racial melting pot. But although social imagery in Brazil includes whites, Indians, and descendents of African-born blacks in their melting pot, in Argentina only Europeans were to be found. According to the official version, because Argentines descended from ships, they have no Indian blood. This regime of diversity invisibility explains the public uproar that followed a historian's statement that General San Martín was the son of a Guaraní Indian.[2] Popular versions that include Indian blood in the Argentine racial mix—abundant in a number of provinces—were made invisible by the overwhelmingly dominant port city myth of Argentines as descendents of ships travelers.

There is a consensus among anthropologists (Briones 1998; Guber 1997; Segato 1998) that the point of departure for cultural homogenization in Argentina is the period between 1880 and 1930, when the modern nation-state was constructed. The degree of synchrony or asynchrony existing between nation building and the process of racial erasure, however, is debatable, as is whether the nation-building period constitutes the real key to this deethnicizing dynamic at all. Be that as it may, what is not in doubt is that in the 1940s ethnic cleavage was irrelevant in national politics. The conflict between Peronist and anti-Peronist forces dominated the political arena during the import-substitution years, and the performability of the myth of Argentine cultural homogeneity implies that ethnicity had not been articulated in political terms at the time as it had in other Latin American countries.

In Argentina a deethnicizing process took place that resulted in "the nation being constructed in such a way that the State became the great antagonist of minorities" (Segato 1998, 183; cf. Briones 1998). Ethnically marked persons were pressured by the state "to shift categories as the only way to enjoy full citizenship rights" (Segato 1998, 183). Antidotes to diversity included the white dust coat worn over regular clothes by public school children, the prohibition against using indigenous languages, universal conscription, and the restriction against giving babies names considered foreign.

Being a foreigner implied different things. Considered a civilizing force, foreigners enjoyed certain privileges over native-born Argentines. But they were also more likely to suffer political persecution and were the butt of ethnic jokes and other stigmatizing mechanisms as well. The medium- and long-range tendency was a growing ethnic erasure from one generation to the next, accompanied by a promise of equality as a reward for accepting cultural guidelines defined as "Argentine."

Pressure on the part of the state to get the nation to behave as an ethnic unit, in conjunction with its power over social inclusion, resulted in ethnic differences and particularities being perceived negatively, if at all. As long as things went well, any mention of ethnicity in political terms was prohibited, or at least discouraged institutionally. Social conflict, structured around the persistent dichotomy between Buenos Aires and the provinces, came to have a political language of its own, according to a number of researchers (Guber 1997; Segato 1998; Neiburg 1997). It is not that European immigrants failed to elicit xenophobic reactions but rather that they received more benefits from the state than internal immigrants migrating from the provinces to Buenos Aires (Halperín Donghi 1987). When they were attacked by the state, it was as socialists and anarchists organizing workers.

This should not be taken to indicate that cultural equality was achieved and that there were no racist constructions in Argentina. What it does mean is that Argentine racist constructions "are not easy to find equivalents for in the way the term 'black' is used in other contexts" (Briones 1998, 23). One example is *cabecita negra*. When the import-substitution economic model stimulated migration from rural to urban areas in the early 1930s, this stigmatizing formula was used by the upper and middle classes to refer to the migratory masses. As we pointed out earlier, in Argentina *negro* is not related to phenotypical features associated with Africa. In everyday speech *negro* or *cabecita negra* was used to refer to someone who was poor (thus preserving the myth that Argentina was a country without blacks).

This usage, which mingles social connotations with cultural ones, obviously has racist overtones. What is peculiarly Argentine is that for long decades, racist terminology was used to indicate a political operation, as Ratier (1971) pointed out many years ago. The dark-skinned provincial workers became synthesized in a political identity: Peronism. The term *cabecita negra* contained "the political nuance that put the sting in the quasi racist confrontation between Buenos Aires dwellers and people from the provinces: to be '*negro*' was to be Peronist and vice versa" (Ratier 1971, 13; see Guber and Visacovsky 1998). Organized on the basis of the invisibility of provincial diversity, here what we term the "field of interlocution" acquired markedly political characteristics.

The concept "field of interlocution" makes it possible to understand how a nation that is not homogeneous nevertheless has a specific and narrow kind of heterogeneous organization. Our hypothesis is that in Argentina the national field of interlocution changed. The term is taken to mean a social and symbolic space within which a set of actors interact, thus recognizing in "others"—including people considered adversaries or enemies—a necessary interlocutor. Only those actors with an identity accepted in the field of interlocution can interact in it. Identifications not entitled to intervene will be incomprehensible to participants in any social dialogue or conflict.

To reiterate, we are not saying that Argentina actually was culturally homogeneous but rather saying that the cultural diversity that was made invisible in social life appeared in full force in Argentina's political life. One example: indigenous invisibility cannot be accounted for demographically because, in proportional terms, Argentina has more persons considered "Indians" than Brazil.[3] By the same token, the lack of visibility of border immigrants as such cannot be solely attributed to demographic factors, because from 1869 to the present day they have constituted between 2 and 3 percent of the total population. Reasons must therefore be sought in historical-social processes.

THE SOUTHERN CONE MIGRATORY SYSTEM: HAS THERE BEEN A SOCIODEMOGRAPHIC CHANGE?

The movement of people within the Southern Cone has a long history. Balán (1992) pointed out the existence of a "Southern Cone migratory system." Traditionally Argentina has attracted immigrants from neighboring countries. Other Southern Cone countries—Paraguay, Uruguay, and Bolivia—have historically been abandoned by citizens who seek their fortune elsewhere. Chile has gone from a country from which people emigrated—many Chileans having come to Argentina—to one that has attracted a growing number of immigrants in recent years. Border migration constitutes one part of a complex regional system that also includes immigration from European and Asian countries, as well as increasing emigration to developed countries (see Oteiza, Novick, and Aruj 1997; Cerruti and Grimson 2005).

In sociodemographic terms, although there have been changes in border migration patterns, this does not necessarily mean that there has been an increase in the number of border migrants. No serious researcher has postulated a doubling of the average number of migrants during the 1990s, for example. On the contrary, such assertions have been debunked by investigators in the field (e.g., Torrado; Benencia).

Percentage of People Born in Neighboring Countries Who
Are Living in Argentina, According to Census Figures

Year	Percent Born in Bordering Countries
1869	2.4
1893	2.9
1914	2.6
1947	2.0
1960	2.3
1970	2.3
1980	2.7
1991	2.6
2001	2.8

Source: INDEC, National Population Censuses, 1869–2001.

The above data is relevant to the debate on whether unemployment is caused by the migratory process, because the rise in the former exceeds by far the rise in the latter. In 1991 border immigrants made up less than 3 percent of the population, whereas the unemployment rate was well above 5 percent. For migration to have caused unemployment—which by 1996 had risen to more than 17 percent—the number of immigrants would have had to triple in five years, which clearly did not happen. According to Benencia and Gazzotti (1995), "the impact of border immigrants in the job market of Buenos Aires and Greater Buenos Aires was slight in global terms." Between October 1992 and October 1994, "the unemployment in greater Buenos Aires went from 6.7 to 13.1% and rose in all urban areas from 7.0 to 12.2 percent." Eliminating the total number of immigrants "who established themselves in the area in the last five years, the October, 1994 unemployment rate would have been reduced by only 1.3%. But if only border immigrants were eliminated, the decrease in the unemployment rate would have been less than 1%" (Benencia and Gazzotti 1995).

Although almost 80,000 immigrants settled in Buenos Aires and greater Buenos Aires between 1989 and 1994, constituting 9.5 percent of the total foreign population, from 1993 to 1998 there were only 54,764 new immigrants, making up only 6.3 percent of the total foreign population. In 1998, in the same metropolitan area, there were only 5,546 more foreigners than in 1994; in addition, the number of new immigrant job seekers older than age 14 years had decreased. So clearly immigrant pressure on the job market had been reduced (INDEC 1999).

Within the category of border immigrants, however, there have been three relevant sociodemographic changes. In the first place, the proportion of border immigrants to the total foreign immigrant population has increased steadily in recent decades, whereas the proportion of Europeans has tended to decline. In fact in recent years 90 percent of the immigrants entering Argentina come from Mercosur member countries or from Chile and Bolivia, which have special accords with Mercosur. Second, instead of settling in remote areas of the country as they used to, border immigrants in recent decades have increasingly come to live in major metropolitan areas; in the 1980s and 1990s, metropolitan Buenos Aires had the highest proportion of border immigrants in the country. And third, the distribution by nationality of immigrants from border countries and from Peru has changed. The number of Uruguayans and Chileans has dropped. In the first case the decline has been from 17 to 12 percent of the total number of immigrants from border countries and from Peru, and in the second case it declined from 30 to 21 percent of immigrants from Uruguay and Chile. In addition, immigration from Peru, a new phenomenon, has reached 9 percent, and immigration from Bolivia has jumped from 18 to 23 percent. Nevertheless, it should be kept in mind that, out of a total population of 36 million, these changes have occurred in a sector of the population numbering around one million persons.

So, as we have seen, although border country immigrants were becoming more visible, this process was insufficient for them to be singled out by ethnic discrimination. Without other, more profound sociocultural changes, there is no reason why these people couldn't have kept on being considered *cabecitas negras* or *villeros* (shantytown dwellers), in accordance with traditional class and race prejudice in Argentina.

An unprecedented phenomenon has appeared in recent anthropological studies: the category of *Boliviano* is commonly used in a number of cities to refer not only to people born in Bolivia but also to their children who, though born in Argentina and therefore legally Argentine, are still considered socially Bolivian. Something very similar is occurring to the Argentine children of Chilean immigrants in certain areas of Patagonia. Public schoolteachers consider the children Chilean, and the children echo the identification (Trpin 2004). Extremely relevant to ethnic visibility, this process indicates that the generational ethnic erasure that characterized Argentina in the past is no longer happening in the case of these children, who have inherited the stigmatized identifications of their parents. This makes it necessary to take another look at the census data. Because if border migrants' children are added to the historic 3 percent of border migrants entering the country, the percentage may be doubled.

Also relevant in this regard is the fact that in certain contexts poor people traditionally referred to as *negros* are now generically called *bolivianos*. In addition the fans of Argentina's most popular soccer team are called *bolivianos* by their main adversary. If earlier Bolivians were added to the category of *negros* that was used to refer to the Argentine poor, now the term *bolivianos* is, in certain contexts, used categorically for the same sector. This makes more comprehensive the perception that Argentina has more border immigrants than in the 1990s. The severity of the metaphor is also eloquent: the poor are turned into "foreigners." Although affirming that Argentina had entered the first world, neoliberal national imagery denationalizes its social effects.

The next question is why the term *boliviano* and not *chileno* or *uruguayo* has been chosen for "foreignizing" poor people. In a country like Argentina, which likes to think of itself as a European enclave in South America with neither *negros* nor Indians, immigrants from the Bolivian altiplano, or their children, call up an indigenous otherness that could not be further from Buenos Aires's self-image: compared with Paraguayans or Chileans—not to mention the Uruguayans—Bolivians are at the bottom of the ethnic hierarchy. In this sense, identifying the poor with Bolivians—as soccer fans do—is a way of making explicit a new type of social and symbolic distance in Argentine intergroup relations.

There has been another significant social change concerning work. Traditionally border migrants tended to occupy labor niches disdained by Argentines. First they came as farm laborers for seasonal work close to the border—Chileans in Patagonia, Bolivians in the northwest, and Paraguayans in the northeast—as a response to labor shortages in the primary sector of the economy (Balán 1990, 271). Then, becoming aware of job opportunities in Buenos Aires, seasonal migrants began to stay on in the 1960s, taking advantage of the chronic shortage of workers for unskilled, unstable, physically demanding jobs (Balán 1990). Most border migrants worked in construction or as domestics.[4] Thus border immigration has contributed historically to overcoming the unskilled labor shortage that characterized the Argentine job market. In other words, migrant labor played a complementary, not competitive, role in the Argentine job market (Mármora 1994).

But what happens when the job situation changes drastically, as we showed in chapter 3? In our view the claims of massive border immigration should be read, instead, as a response to massive unemployment; what has changed is not the number of immigrants but rather the job prospects for Argentines. The latter, who never accepted the working conditions that immigrants did, will now take any job regardless of working conditions. Social exclusion processes—along with the noticeable increase in unemployment that aggravates job competition—have made jobs traditionally held by border immigrants desirable to recently impoverished sectors of the population.

In summary, *it is not that immigrants have begun to compete with Argentines for jobs; instead, Argentines are the ones now competing with immigrants for jobs they used to disdain.* In a word, what has changed is not the volume of immigration but rather Argentina itself. Even before the consequences of this change were assumed ideologically and culturally, a new frontier had formed: the frontier between Argentines on one side, and Bolivians and Paraguayans—the border immigrants—on the other.

This new frontier is based on the old distinction according to which Argentina did not belong to Latin America—and should do everything possible to remain in a category all its own. This, however, contradicted the grandiose Mercosur project.

CHANGES IN THE ETHNIC VISIBILITY REGIME

Transformations in socioeconomic and sociopolitical condition bring about innovations in the ways social actors are identified and interact with each other. These changes show up in the modes and categories used in the field of interlocution, where long-forgotten patterns of identification reappear and the terms of identity are once more the subject of dispute.

Among the changes occurring in the field of interlocution in Argentina is the reappearance of certain categories that had been rendered invisible during the nationalization process: aborigine; *negro* (meaning black, not poor); and border immigrant groups. They began to reemerge as key tools for mobilizing broad sectors of Argentine society. The increased organizational efforts and activism on the part of these groups has been analyzed in a number of research projects and case studies on immigrants, native people, and Afro-Argentine organizations. First appearing in the 1980s and gaining momentum in the 1990s, new cleavages in identity categories appeared, and a growing ethnic differentiation, in terms of discrimination and xenophobia as well as ethnic self-assertion, became politically relevant.

XENOPHOBIA

In the 1990s two waves of xenophobic discourse went beyond the everyday discriminatory mechanisms experienced by border immigrants. Because the ebb and flow of border migration depends, in large part, on economic dynamics, there is bound to be some correlation between periods of economic expansion in Argentina and the influx of new immigrants on one hand and recessionary periods and their return to their country of origin on the other. And it is precisely during recessions that xenophobes attribute increases in unemployment and delinquency to the immigrants. This correlation shows how little relevance the actual number of immigrants has in xenophobic campaigns and how great the government's need to find a scapegoat in times of crisis is. So it is not surprising that xenophobic waves arose at times—the second half of the 1990s—when, in all probability, immigrants were returning to their countries of origin.

During these years government officials played key roles in the xenophobia wave, placing the responsibility for social, economic, sanitary, and security problems on immigrants (see Oteiza, Novick, and Aruj 1997). Foreign Minister Guido Di Tella's prediction that "in the year 2020, 20% of the Argentine population will be Bolivians and Paraguayans,"[5] accompanied an identity politics best synthesized in two statements by the same minister: "We want to be near the rich and the beautiful"[6] and "We don't want to be with the horrible people." Thus it was that border migration undermined the Argentine elite's mythology that they lived in a Europeanized enclave in Latin America.

In June 1995 Eduardo Duhalde, the governor of the province of Buenos Aires at the time, launched a two-pronged employment plan to pave streets and rout out undocumented workers in defense of Argentine jobs. "In my province jobs are for Argentines or foreigners legally residing in the country." Given that the paperwork involved in gaining legal residence in Argentina is long and complicated, for all practical purposes this meant that jobs were for Argentines and long-established, not recent, immigrants. In this regard part of Duhalde's plan consisted of inspecting establishments that hired foreigners and sending undocumented workers back to their countries of origin.[7] At the same time, Governor Duhalde worked to pass a law that would allow foreigners to vote in provincial elections, with polls showing more than 50 percent of them favoring the Peronist party. In February 1999 Duhalde insisted, "There is less and less work, and it must be shared out among Argentines" (*Clarín*, February 14, 1999). A few days later President Carlos Menem stated, "People without proper documentation will have to abandon the country" (*Clarín*, February 14, 1999).

The Construction Workers' Union (*Unión Obrera de la Construcción* or UOCRA) added its voice to the xenophobic campaign. It claimed that the responsibility for the lack of jobs, on-the-job accidents, and low wages belonged not to the government, business, or labor but rather to the *bolitas* and *paraguas*—derogatory names for Bolivians and Paraguayans, respectively—who stole jobs from Argentine workers. The union then demanded from the government stricter control over illegal immigration and more severe penalties for undocumented border immigrants.

After a number of fatal on-the-job accidents, on August 5, 1998, the UOCRA held a demonstration, attended by more than ten thousand construction workers, protesting against unsafe working conditions that were costing the lives of an average of 85 workers a month. Because unsafe working conditions do not discriminate against any one nationality, Bolivian workers attended the demonstration. But they were obliged to march in a separate column along with Peruvians and Paraguayans, who were also discriminated against by their fellow workers. From the mainstream column, chants such as

"We are Argentines and Peronists" and "We are Argentines and not *bolitas* [Bolivians]" were heard. A worker stated to a newspaper reporter, "They [foreigners] are to blame for us earning less and less" (*Clarín*, June 6, 1998).

During the xenophobic wave in early 1999, the subject of delinquency and the lack of security assumed unprecedented importance, which took the form of strong declarations by high government officials, increased police action against immigrants, and the presentation in the national congress of a number of bills restricting immigration. In mid-January the federal police allegedly reported a significant increase in the number of foreigners involved in urban crime. During the same period of time, a district attorney for the city of Buenos Aires indicated that foreigners committed only 10 percent of the petty crime in the city. However, Secretary of Migrations Hugo Franco affirmed that immigrants committed 60 percent of all petty crimes: "Crime in the federal capital has become foreignized," he declared. For his part, Minister of the Interior Carlos Corach stated that 56 percent of the people arrested for all kinds of crime were foreigners (*Clarín*, January 21, 1999). Against a backdrop of recession, a campaign to arrest illegal immigrants was launched: more than 1,100 undocumented persons were arrested in nineteen days at one Buenos Aires police station (*Clarín*, January 21, 1999).[8] The Argentine president stated, "Undocumented persons will have to leave the country," because Argentina closes its door to "people who come to commit crimes against our nation." He went on to say, "If one asks illegal immigrants to get their papers in order, the subject of human rights comes up right away" (*Clarín*, January 21, 1999).

The government then sent a bill to Congress asking for greater control over illegal immigration, stiffer penalties for persons helping them enter the country, and sanctions against firms employing them, as well as more facilities for expelling them. The bill also gave the executive branch the power to establish the criteria for admitting foreigners and deciding how long they could stay.

During the same period of time, the supposed increase in crimes committed by foreigners alluded to by government officials was denied by the federal police. Commissioner Major Roberto Galvarino, general director of the Urban Order Department, stated, "The participation of immigrants in assaults, robberies and homicides is slight. Although statistics are not kept, we suppose it to be around 5 to 7%" (*Clarín,* January 21, 1999).

Figures for *arrests* were intentionally confused with those for *convictions.* Those arrested are "suspected" of having committed a crime, whereas those convicted have been proved guilty in a court of law; the police make the arrest, but guilt can be established only by the justice system. In the institutions responsible, the idea that "an immigrant is suspicious by definition" and "immigrants commit crimes" predominated. By arresting immigrants for looking like immigrants, their very actions distorted the real situation. Figures for 1994 indicate that almost 90 percent of those convicted of a crime were Argentines, the figure rising to almost 95 percent for violent crimes. The figure corresponding to white-collar crime—fraud, fraudulent bankruptcy, extortion—is almost 100 percent (Mármora 1994). By the same token, according to statistics from the Subsecretariat for Population of the Ministry of the Interior, "the percentage of foreigners convicted of crimes is 4.6%" (Mármora 1999).

Nevertheless, the xenophobic discourse had an effect on a large part of the population. According to a poll taken in 1996, the two groups arousing the greatest distrust among Argentines were Bolivians (55 percent) and Chileans (58 percent).[9] "81% of the population seems to agree that foreign workers should be limited in number. 91% think that immigration hurts Argentines, and half of the persons consulted favor expelling 'illegal immigrants' from Latin American countries" (Oteiza and Aruj 1995).

In a survey taken by the Center for Public Opinion Studies, 63 percent of those interviewed answered affirmatively when asked if they thought Argentines were racists (*Clarín,* April 26, 1998). The same survey found that "Bolivians are the main victims of this discrimination, followed very closely by dark-skinned Argentines." Of the 63 percent that considered Argentines racist, 50.5 percent thought that "Argentines don't like Bolivians." On the other hand, 75 percent of those interviewed thought that foreigners diminished the possibility of Argentines' finding a job. And finally, a survey conducted by the Union Center of Studies for a New Majority, coordinated by Rosendo Fraga, found that 77 percent of those polled thought that greater control should be exercised over immigration (*Tres Puntos,* February 10, 1999).

These statistics depict the conflict occurring in everyday intercultural relations. On the job, in the street, on the bus, Bolivians perceive they "are viewed with distrust" or insulted (see Grimson 1999). In public schools in Buenos Aires, for example, teachers have constructed stereotypes and stigmas regarding the ethnic, national, and class origins of their students. Bolivians or Bolivians' children are categorized as "slow, lazy, quiet," and positively as "humble, respectful, well-behaved." The teachers in one school described them as follows: "They are still coming down out of the hills, and they don't arrive until they're in the fifth grade," thus combining in a single cultural stereotype environmental determinism, along with predictions of intellectual capacity and expected behavior. This, in an educational context, can be described as a "self-fulfilling prophecy" (Sinisi 1998).

There were some academics, human rights organizations, and religious sectors that, from a universalist perspective, attempted to counter the stigmatizing of immigrants as "inferior" and "dangerous." In addition Bolivians were valued in certain business sectors for working long hours and causing few problems. This made Bolivians sought after by the garment industry and as truck gardeners, for example.

Considered as a whole, xenophobic manifestations and acts did not reach the pitch in Argentina that they did in other countries, especially European ones. Although there were, and still are, situations of exclusion and even physical violence, no organized general movement against immigrants arose. However, in the late 1990s, such a possibility did not seem all that remote.

THE CHANGING ROLE OF ETHNICITY

The official and unofficial insistence on nationality as the basis for granting civil and political rights, as well as the positive view of nationality in other contexts, had a correlation in the organizing activity of migratory groups. The tendency—among some immigrant groups at any rate—was to regroup around ethnic identity. In other words, in a hostile environment in which an exclusion dynamic made it impossible to articulate any broader social identity, migrant groups exhibited a tendency toward ever-greater ethnic-national identification. This included institutional activities that ran the gamut from celebrating national holidays, putting on fairs, and organizing football leagues to creating civil organizations and federations to fight for migrants' rights.

The following is a brief indication of these processes in migrant, indigenous, and Afro-Argentine groups. Border migrants have represented between 2 and 3 percent of the Argentine population in each and every national census from the nineteenth century to date (INDEC 1996). But not until the 1990s were several hundred new border immigrant organizations formed, including federations made up of Bolivian, Paraguayan, and Chilean groups. In addition, the Latin American Confederation of Collectivities and Communities was founded. In the absence of a drastic demographic change, what are the factors bringing about this organizational surge in border migrants? Although it is too early for a definitive answer, we should note that these organizations and federations arose in the context of increasingly broad-based civil, cultural, and athletic organizations (Pereyra 2001) as well as a stronger presence of migrants in public spaces.

Regarding Bolivians, there has been a gradual increase in their organizing activities beginning in the 1970s. In 1975 they began to celebrate Bolivia's patron saint's day as a community. During the 1980s the number of festivals, fairs, and radio programs grew. In the mid-1990s two FM stations dedicated to "maintaining traditions" were established, and a Federation of Bolivian Civil Associations was formed to establish relations with the Argentine government and the Bolivian embassy in Argentina. This network grew up out of the need to institute channels for claiming civil rights that included not only equal access to work, health care, and education but also the right to cultural differentiation (Grimson 1999). Chileans and Paraguayans also created a joint federation and achieved certain political goals. Although the Paraguayans who didn't find the new accord beneficial succeeded in stopping its being signed (Halpern 1999), the Chileans fought for and got the right to vote for foreigners in the province of Buenos Aires (Pereyra 2001). At a later date Peruvians also created organizations and ways to show "their culture" in public (Benza 2002). They have also organized to demand certain rights such as access to the university for undocumented persons and better access to Argentine documentation processes (Canevaro 2004).

This increase in the organizing activity of border migrants took place within the framework of a more general process of change in the ways in which individuals and groups perceived their own identity. In an analysis of the cultural relations between different sectors of "black culture" in Buenos Aires, Frigerio (2000a) found a similar tendency:

> Until recently Afro-Argentines, with no clear visibility, had lost their capacity to present their own version of their culture and patrimony. They had been replaced by Afro-Uruguayans, with a long history and strong public presence, and by the practitioners of Afro-Brazilian religions as representatives of their own history and tradition. Nevertheless, in the last two years, a group of Afro-Argentines has created an organization called *Africa Vive* that has attempted to recover a certain visibility for them.

A number of indigenous groups have also sought to increase their organizational presence and public image in Argentina (Hirsch 2000a; Vázquez 2000; Escolar 2000). The construction of their ethnicity should be understood and viewed as a strategy for increasing their political participation.[10] The processes of "emergence"—or ethnicization of indigenous groups—have occurred both in their area of origin and in the urban areas where they have migrated.

In sum, a great number of factors indicate important transformations occurring in the Argentine field of interlocution. Categories of identification appeared or reappeared that have brought about qualitative changes in traditional relations and social conflict in Argentina. On the other hand, tendencies toward cultural fundamentalism were also consolidated (Stolcke 1999) that may deepen and broaden present-day discrimination and segregation. Significant in this regard is the fact that, along with the increase in ethnic organizations, the Argentine state began new discriminatory practices. In official discourse and regulations regarding the entry and documentation of migrants, the state increasingly used nationality as a political argument to justify establishing differential rights (Oteiza, Novick, and Aruj 1997; Grimson 2000a). In this sense, as xenophobic manifestations increased and border migrants could no longer escape detection, new forms of social organization were needed to publicly revindicate a specific ethnicity.

Any comparison of discrimination and segregation practices based on ethnicity between Argentina and the United States shows a much greater fluidity and porosity in the former country. This is not surprising, because social relations were never structured around slavery and because ethnic-racial neighborhoods or ghettos did not grow up in Argentine cities. Nevertheless, as we showed, a growing cleavage, differentiation, and even residential segregation, characterized the 1990s in Argentina.

THE IMPASSE IN 2002

One interesting element regarding the image of Argentine migrants is the historical nature of the relations among different sociocultural groups. The 2001–2002 social and economic crisis marked a before and an after in the national social, political, and cultural imagery regarding immigration in Argentina: whereas before the crisis it was possible to affirm that Bolivian, Paraguayan, and Peruvian immigrants signaled Argentina's entry into the first world, such a statement is totally implausible today as new social narratives appear.

In the darkest moments of the crisis, the press reported that border migrants were returning to their native countries. Although the number of departing migrants was small, occurring as it did at a time when unemployment was rising steeply, the exodus made blaming unemployment on border migrants less plausible than before. The crisis was so strong and deep that border migrants, either by returning to their native countries or by surviving as best they could alongside their Argentine neighbors, could no longer be made the scapegoat for high unemployment and crime rates.

We discussed earlier one example of this change in attitude: the former governor of the province of Buenos Aires, Eduardo Duhalde, who employed xenophobic, nationalistic rhetoric against illegal immigrants and was in favor of jobs for Argentines. In 2002 he became the president of Argentina, and during the year and a half he was in office, he did not mention illegal immigration a single time. The same person who had scapegoated illegal immigration in the 1990s to justify public policy in the face of growing problems was now operating in a completely different context, and he did not touch on the subject. In 2002, with the real causes so painfully apparent, nobody in his right mind would have believed for a minute that border migration was responsible for high unemployment. And this is precisely why the same government officials that had led the xenophobic campaign in the mid-1990s made no mention of illegal immigration when they once more found themselves in high places in 2001.

This related to a more general transformation in the ways immigrants are perceived by society at large. Two opinion polls bear witness to the change that occurred between 1999 and 2002. In answer to the question of whether they favored limiting immigration and shortening the period of time immigrants were allowed to remain in the country, 77 percent answered affirmatively in 1999, whereas only 51 percent did in 2002. And although only 18 percent opposed greater restrictions on immigration in 1999, 42 percent were against them in 2002. Regarding whether restricting immigration would help solve the insecurity problem, opinion in 1999 was evenly divided, with 45 percent saying yes and 46 percent, saying no. In 2002, 77 percent did not think more restrictions would help, and 18 percent thought they would (Casaravilla 2003). Clearly, the place border immigrants occupied in Argentine social imagery in the 1990s changed when the way Argentines perceived themselves changed, as they did after the 2001–2002 crisis.

Border immigrants also changed their way of interacting in public during this time. During the worst moments of the crisis, they made no specific demands. Actually, in the early months of 2002, any purely corporative demand would have been out of place, because all political energy was being devoted to the basic needs of food and work. The crisis affected ethnic corporativism: how can "minority" demands be advanced when the viability of the country as a whole is at stake?

Thus it was that ethnicized demands disappeared in 2002; as indigenous groups marched with *piqueteros* in the city of

Buenos Aires, Paraguayan and Bolivian migrants joined different movements of the unemployed and, in some cases, became important figures in the social struggle for employment plans or in reopening closed factories and making them operational. This time around they hid their ethnicity, becoming basically just one more neighbor or fellow worker.

With regard to organized labor, although chants accusing border immigrants of "stealing jobs" were heard during demonstrations in the 1990s, in 2002 the unemployed formed neighborhood groups with no distinction made for national origin. Paraguayan and Bolivian immigrants marched with *piqueteros,* at times representing the entire group in organizations for the unemployed.

Of course this should not be taken to mean everyday discrimination against border immigrants in Argentinan has come to an end. What it does mean is that ethnic stigmatizing became—temporarily at least—much less relevant than it had been in the 1990s. Although the reappearance of an ethnicizing dynamic in the future cannot be ruled out, we want to stress that during the worst moments of the crisis, between 2001 and 2002, a change occurred in Argentine social imagery that has affected the way border migrants are perceived. If in the 1990s they confirmed Argentines' view of their country as a European enclave, after 2001 the official discourse shifted to the desire "to be a normal country." Above and beyond the polysemy of the formula, there is no doubt that in Argentina all pretensions to power and first-world status have been definitively laid to rest. By the same token, for economic and political reasons, Argentina finds itself farther from the United States and closer to its neighbors, to whom it no longer takes for granted its superiority.

We now want to sketch out what we consider a series of relatively well-articulated economic, social, and identificatory phases. Import substitution ended up associated with the political cleavage of Peronism and anti-Peronism, which absorbed existing ethnic-racial tensions, along with the historical cleavage of the provinces of Buenos Aires. The segmentation and fragmentation characterizing the neoliberal phase diluted traditional political identifications, and new ethnicizing dynamics appeared in certain specific sectors. The crisis in the neoliberal economic model, new social articulations, and changes in the political value of ethnicity do not mean that the migrant organizations created and consolidated during the 1990s have disappeared or been substantially weakened. In the context of the new situation that has opened up, these organizations will be social actors, although their role has changed in part.

Within this framework, in which, as we showed in chapter 1, Argentina is seeking to redefine its place in Latin America, there arises the possibility that not only the marketplace will be regionalized but the workforce will be as well. This is because any project postulating social inclusion and less social inequality as necessary conditions for sustaining a democratic form of government will find it hard to propose anything less than regional citizenship rights.

Paradoxically, the movement of large groups of people who are habitually associated with globalization and regionalization processes would seem to relegate thousands of men and women to a fourth world with no citizenship rights whatsoever. What this means is that Southern Cone countries will increasingly find themselves at a crossroads in coming years. One possibility is that border migrant citizenship rights will be further reduced, increasing illegality, xenophobic campaigns, and social exclusion. In this scenario, border migration will not stop, but new immigrants will live clandestinely with no social or political rights whatsoever. Unfortunately, this dark future is not implausible.

But, based on the declarations of brotherhood heard at Mercosur encounters, another road is possible. It will require the rejection of the narrowly nationalistic policies that the rejection and marginality of border immigrants rests on. It will require comprehending that regionalization can bring about not only economic development but integral human development as well. As graffiti painted on a wall in a Buenos Aires neighborhood so eloquently put it: "No human being is illegal" (Beltrán and Reges 2003). Furthermore, if public policy and regional accords do not emphasize granting full social and cultural rights to all Southern Cone citizens, then regional economic development will lack the necessary social underpinnings to make it viable in the long run.

Neoliberalism was not just government policy. It was a constellation of sociocultural patterns and practices that transformed how Argentines imagined themselves and their country and how they interacted socially and politically with each other and the nation itself. It is also important to remember that the first phase of neoliberal reform (1990–96) had broad, albeit not monolithic, public support.

How to explain the existence of this consensus in the first place, how it held up long after the effects of neoliberal shock policies were felt, and how popular sectors of Argentine society continued to legitimize the very policies that hurt them were questions that obsessed social scientists during the 1990s. Following Navarro (1995), one factor was undoubtedly the fear of the return of hyperinflation, which had created a consensus for "running with the ball no matter what" to avoid economic chaos, regardless of future consequences. Other investigators saw in the policies in question an astute combination of manipulation, co-optation, and repression that made economic adjustment palatable (see Acuña and Smith 1994). According to yet another hypothesis, like those in certain developed countries that had gained a consensus for reducing the welfare state, Argentines were willing to accept the relative privation and sacrifice demanded by neoliberal policies as the price to be paid to ensure a better future (Przeworski 1991). Also, the identity crisis that fragmented the population into ever-smaller groups helped legitimize reduced government spending because, since sacrifice was relative, some interest groups always received favorable treatment (Offe 1987).

But in retrospect it is as erroneous to allege the existence of a uniform consensus favoring neoliberal reform over the course of a decade as it is to affirm that neoliberal policies were passively accepted across the board by Argentine society. Little by little the view that neoliberalism was "the only possible alternative" began to crack, and new social and political initiatives questioning its policies and seeking to deal with their effects arose as the decade wore on. They grew in number and gained adherents across an ever-broader social spectrum between 1996 and 1997, with activity peaking in 2001 and 2002.

Of course this social mobilization did not occur in a vacuum. Argentina, which is a country with a long associative tradition, had one of the highest percentages of trade union membership in the world; community improvement organizations have always been an important force for progress in working-class neighborhoods, and cooperatives of different kinds have strong roots in rural and urban areas of the country. Even though the last military dictatorship decimated a generation of social leaders, diverse forms of resistance to state terrorism did arise before it fell. And afterward, with the return of constitutional government in the 1980s, social mobilization on human rights issues, labor questions, and education and housing matters was massive and intense.

Possibly it is against this backdrop that the early 1990s came to be diagnosed early on as a time of social dearticulation. But such a judgment was premature at best. Social action is cyclical, and certainly it is not surprising that the period of protest and innovation that grew up around 1996 and 1997 followed upon a seemingly passive prior stage, during which time forces regrouped, collective identities were reshaped, and new ground was broken. As has been well-demonstrated by Hirschmann (1970), passive periods do not necessarily mean protest has died out; they are instead simply one more stage in the continuous ebb and flow of focusing on private concerns and collective action.

The contrast between the 1970s and the 1990s is indeed striking, and not only with regard to the drawing power of radical ideology in the two eras. Between the two decades social protagonists had changed, and of course so had the type of social demands set forth and the actions conceived of to satisfy them. Broadly speaking, the locus of collective action shifted from production-related sectors like labor unions to the arena of social reproduction, which was centered around the neighborhood and community. By the same token, demands for better salaries and working conditions were replaced by the demand for simple inclusion—jobs—and the wherewithal to satisfy basic needs, meaning food. Marches to the Plaza de Mayo, which lies before the seat of the federal government, the Casa Rosada (the paradigmatic final destination for protest demonstrations in Argentina), were complemented, and at times replaced, by other forms of social action. Social protest became decentralized: individual provinces, communities, and neighborhoods turned into the sites where social conflicts occurred, at times with national repercussions.

To better comprehend the changes occurring in the way social discontent manifested itself, we take a brief look at the role of labor unions in Argentine political life. The fact that they were a key player until the 1990s was not an accident but rather a direct consequence of the special relationship that grew out of the relationship between the state and labor unions under Peronism: the latter, referred to as the "spinal column of the Peronist movement," provided political legitimacy and votes in exchange for social benefits for union members. Labor continued playing a leading role when democracy was restored in 1983 and a non-Peronist government took office. During the Alfonsín presidency (1983–89), the umbrella labor organization (or CGT [National Confederation of Workers]) called 13 general strikes. But when Carlos Menem, a Peronist, took office and implemented neoliberal reform, he did so with the CGT's blessing, in spite of the loss of an unprecedented number of workers' rights gained after long struggle over the years. With high-ranking union officials holding important positions in the Menem government, negotiations centered around how to employ union social security funds, the source of the political and economic power these same officials wielded. During this same period, unemployment tripled and then quadrupled. The turning point was a wave of strikes and demonstrations protesting the privatizing of state enterprises and the dismissal of workers in 1990. After that, the big labor unions, whose membership was declining, decided the best policy was to let themselves be co-opted.

The human rights movement was the other force capable of mobilizing large groups of people in Argentina. During the 1980s thousands of people marched, demanding that all those guilty of torturing people and making people disappear during the preceding military dictatorship be tried in a court of law. The pardon granted to military chiefs by the Menem government in 1990 in the face of massive protests closed the decade and marked the end of an era.

No single force would again articulate a social movement as labor unions and human rights organizations had in their day. In the 1990s social protest was highly fragmented and short-lived. Labor unrest was limited to the service sector and government employees. To be sure, there were popular uprisings against the abuses of quasi-feudal power exercised by provincial governors in northern Argentina. But in general, demands became diversified, with specific things being protested against in specific places. The result was "a high degree of fragmentation and little possibility of constructing a unified subject capable of extending its scope of action in time and space" (Schuster and Pereyra 2001, 59–60).

The general situation at the end of the decade was very different. New social subjects with new identities, such as the *piqueteros,*[1] or people involved in factory takeovers to save their jobs, appeared on the scene. Very different from traditional labor protest, these new social movements also distinguished themselves from the transient, fragmented, single-issue protests of the early part of the decade.[2] Innovations also occurred in the field of human rights. The transnational court struggle to extradite Augusto Pinochet, and the trials held in Europe to bring Argentine human rights violators to justice introduced an international dimension. Also, human rights violators were once again being brought before courts of law in Argentina, and the activity of social actors such as HIJOS (children of the disappeared) and Abuelas de Plaza de Mayo (Plaza de Mayo Grandmothers) placed human rights issues in the public sphere once again, following the crushing defeat signified by the pardons in 1989.

In the final analysis, the retreat in the field of social rights that marked the 1990s was matched by important advances in the rights of individuals and specific groups such as women, ethnic and sexual minorities, and so on. Moreover, not infrequently the same actors—multilateral credit organizations, for example—opposed social rights while working in favor of individual and group ones. In theory, there is no contradiction between neoliberal reforms and individual rights; it can even be argued that a kind of synergy between the two serves to legitimize socioeconomic reform policies. In the real world there is a constant give-and-take between how those who advocate individual rights and those who work to advance social ones understand and put into effect the different aspects of the concept of rights. A discourse defending individual rights may be appropriated by actors to back up their demands for social ones. As well, the two types of rights may be deemed mutually exclusive by institutional actors but complementary for the particular purposes of noninstitutional ones.

This being the case, our next step is to examine the interplay between these factors to understand what happened on the ground in Argentina. A brief synopsis of events follows. There was an initial phase of consensus on neoliberal reform, which extended through the reelection of Carlos Menem in 1995. Then an economic slowdown, which began in 1996, turned into a full-blown recession in the second half of 1998, resulting in increasing unemployment and poverty rates. This, combined with a number of corruption scandals, destroyed the political legitimacy of neoliberal reform in the eyes of most Argentines. The coup de grâce came in December 2001 when, in response to the deep recession, high unemployment, and economic crisis, the government froze bank deposits (the *corralito*). The massive banging of pots and pans—or *cacerolazo*—on December 19, 2001, followed by demonstrations and repression, brought about the resignation of the president on the following day. Between January and March 2002, demonstrations erupted all over Argentina. During December 2001, 859 *cacerolazos* were recorded; there were 706 in January 2002, 310 in February, and only 139 in March. It is highly likely that there were more street demonstrations in 2002 than at any other time during the past fifteen years. Then social activity abruptly dropped off. The low level of social conflict recorded in 2004 marked the end of the high level of social protest against neoliberal reform that had begun in 1996.

Between 1996 and 2003 new types of popular organizations came into being. For example, barter networks appeared, permitting people to exchange goods and services without spending money, and an informal barter circuit grew up that, at its height, involved two million people (Hintze 2003). Neighborhood meal centers, where food was prepared for the indigent and milk and snacks were given to needy children, multiplied, often supplied by municipal governments and private donations. The unemployed also organized themselves into pressure groups for obtaining food and unemployment stipends from the government. In mainly middle-class neighborhoods, public assemblies were held where Argentines, whose "commitment" was not primarily economic—they didn't necessarily have funds frozen in the bank and they weren't indigent or unemployed—gathered to discuss what was to be done in the face of the profound social, political, and institutional crisis. Bankrupt or abandoned factories and other business enterprises were taken over by former employees, who then attempted to get them up and running again and thus save their jobs. Also, concerned groups organized new types of mobilization to protest against urban insecurity.

We now take a close look at particular organizations and movements, whose birth and development has transformed collective imagery and undermined the neoliberal pretension to be the "only alternative."

NEIGHBORHOOD MEAL CENTERS

According to national mythology, at the end of the nineteenth century, Argentina was considered "the breadbasket of the world." As exporters of meat and grain, Argentines were convinced that, unlike their neighbors, nobody went hungry in their country. However, from the 1980s on, hunger has become a major social issue in Argentina. When asked about the *ollas populares,* or common cooking pots to which people contributed what they had, springing up in poor neighborhoods, the social welfare minister of the last military dictatorship, General Navajas Artaza, replied, "Nobody goes hungry in Argentina. The *ollas populares* are pure politics. People do go hungry in the United States too. You can't generalize" (quoted in Hintze 1989). With the inauguration of the National Food Plan when democracy returned less than three years later, 700,000 needy families began receiving monthly packets of food, and the issue of hunger became officially recognized.

That nobody went hungry in Argentina had not been a myth in the past. Differences in nutritional intake between rich and poor were not that different in the 1960s.[3] Although quality differed according to pocketbook, meat, a staple in the Argentine diet, was abundant and cheap enough for everyone to afford. But socioeconomic changes put an end to this "nutritional security" for a substantial sector of the population.[4] Nutritional security entails sufficient food supplies, seasonal stability, national autonomy, long-range sustainability, and equity. This last requirement is the one that stopped being fulfilled, which meant that the problem was not availability but a lack of purchasing power.

Availability was uneven during the last quarter of a century. Oscillations, however, never exceeded 15 percent, which meant that even during critical periods, food was available. But when it came to purchasing power (the relationship between prices and income), the oscillations were severe, with declines of up to 55 percent with regard to the base year (1975). The two sharp, short-lived declines correspond to 1981, the end of the military dictatorship, and 1989 to 1990, the period of hyperinflation. Purchasing power during the 1990s shows two stages: a marked increase between 1991 and 1993, followed by a slow decline that ends up close to the level during hyperinflation in December 2001.[5] Broadly speaking, we can conclude that the market did not encourage or guarantee equity in the food access (Aguirre 2004).

The responses of Argentine society to this nutritional crisis ran from loosely organized initiatives to nationwide campaigns. Beginning at the end of the military dictatorship, women in poor neighborhoods joined together to solicit donations from local businesses and municipal authorities. They sought food donations and, when they were successful, communally cooked and distributed the dishes they prepared equally among their children.

Hunger has had severe political consequences in Argentina. On two occasions, in 1989 and 2001, supermarkets were sacked in urban areas. When nutritional crises occurred in conjunction with political-institutional crises, thousands of people from poor neighborhoods, at times encouraged by community leaders and at times acting on their own initiative, stormed supermarkets, carrying away everything they could. After the 1989 supermarket sacking, then-president Raúl Alfonsín resigned. In 2001 then-president Fernando de la Rúa announced that sackers would be repressed and declared a state of emergency; a broad swath of Buenos Aires's middle-sectors responded by taking to the streets, beating pots and pans in what came to be known as the December 19th *cacerolazo*. The president then resigned. Clearly, hunger and its consequences have far-reaching political repercussions in Argentina.

Although supermarket sackings were exceptional social outbursts that lasted only a few days in 1989 and 2001, organizing common cooking pots and neighborhood meal centers is an everyday occurrence that has tended to persist over time. As unemployment spread in popular neighborhoods in the late 1990s and it became clear that hunger was not a passing phenomenon, the occasional common cooking pot turned into permanent neighborhood meal centers, becoming important community institutions in the process. Local and provincial governments; Caritas, the Catholic Church's charitable organization; other religious groups; retired people's social security organizations; schools; clubs; community organizations; popular assemblies; and organizations of the unemployed (among others) all have become mediating agents for obtaining and collectively distributing food.

Neighborhood food programs often function in conjunction with different government food programs. For example, community organizations from the *villas miseria*, or poor neighborhoods, on the outskirts of the city in greater Buenos Aires can obtain a regular supply of food and funds to buy equipment to prepare it from the city government. There are currently nutritional programs in place for supplying approximately one community meal center for every thousand inhabitants of *villas miseria,* this in a city with two hundred thousand inhabitants living in poor neighborhoods.

Greater Buenos Aires is home to the highest concentration of indigent and poor people in the country. Since the late 1990s, the provincial government has been administering a program, the Life Plan (*Plan Vida*), whose purpose is to coordinate government policy and community initiatives, a secondary function being the establishment of support networks for the governing Justicialist party. The mainstay of the program is local women from poor neighborhoods who volunteer to take charge of the nutritional necessities of one block, or *manzana* (and hence the women are called *manzaneras*). This program, which began feeding 50,000 people in 1994, involved more than a million five years later.

The neighborhood meal centers that arose to meet a nutritional emergency and did not disappear became institutionalized. Food procurement and preparation routines were established, requirements for eligibility stipulated, lists of beneficiaries drawn up, and small neighborhood enterprises created that, once their program was approved by the government, could pay staff members. Thus, it was that what had begun as volunteer efforts to form solidarity networks to feed hungry children became places of employment like any other. Over time social emergency measures, workplace routines, and popular neighborhood political networks became intertwined in the neighborhood meal centers.

In short, emergency initiatives to feed the hungry became a key part of government welfare policy in the late 1990s. Members of organizations for the unemployed in greater Buenos Aires have described how local mayors countered their demands for jobs by enumerating the number of neighbor-hood meal centers their city was funding. The unemployed remained unconvinced—"create jobs, not soup kitchens," was their reply. Above and beyond whether this was something mayors could do, the point here is how what was once an emergency measure has become an everyday reality: it has become normal not to have a job and to be fed by government food programs.

BARTER CLUBS

Against a background of growing unemployment and an ever-greater lack of purchasing power, one very creative response to the crisis on the part of civil society was the barter club. In early 2002 the birth of barter clubs, which changed the landscape in a number of cities, made headlines in Argentine papers. People began to frequent barter fairs organized in clubhouses, audi-toriums, and abandoned factories, where they could exchange goods, skills, and knowledge they possessed for something they didn't without the need for money. In no time barter clubs became a sign of hope: a response to the crisis did exist, and what was even better, it came not from the government or inter-national organizations but from the people.

Stories about Argentine barter clubs, which caught the eye of European intellectuals passing through Buenos Aires, appeared in foreign papers.[6] In Argentina the phenomenon generated such enthusiasm that the original barter network was invited to participate in the "Roundtable Dialogue on Argentina," an intersectorial discussion on ways to deal with the crisis.[7]

The first club was created in Bernal, an old industrial area in the southern part of greater Buenos Aires, on May 1,

1995. Its founders were professionals who decided to form a neighborhood group to cultivate home vegetable gardens and exchange produce from home gardens, according to the needs of each family. The group met in a local abandoned textile factory, *La Bernalesa*.

In the beginning, bartering was a strategy employed by the impoverished middle class to mitigate unemployment and deteriorating living conditions. According to the founders of the first club in Bernal, the initiative was inspired by the "Campaign against Hunger" in Brazil, which functioned as a loosely connected group of social institutions and nongovernmental organizations. But because impoverished middle-class members did not go hungry, the objective was, initially, to find alternatives to the formal market economy (see Gonzalez Bombal 2002; Hintze 2003; Luzzi 2005). As the clubs spread, traditionally poor sectors formed their own bartering networks to obtain what they couldn't afford to buy, mainly food.

As networks multiplied, the way bartering was conducted became increasingly complex. Simple exchanges of goods or services between two parties turned into "multireciprocal exchanges" among many people, with the help of a card on which individual transactions were tallied. As the number of participants grew, a nationwide network of barter clubs was formed and a chit system introduced, with one chit worth one Argentine peso in any participating network node.

The number of participants continued growing: in 2001 the number of nodes doubled, with participants numbering 500,000 in more than 20 provinces. In early 2002, in part as a result of the banking crisis that severely reduced circulating currency, 4,500 barter clubs were said to be functioning, involving two million people.

The December 2001 economic collapse had a dual effect on barter clubs: the number of participants expanded greatly, and the network was weakened as the unprecedented popularity of barter clubs brought to light the inherent limitations of the system. The system for issuing chits was complicated from the start. According to the organization charter, after carrying out a given number of transactions, each new member was to receive 50 free chits or *créditos* to stimulate bartering. The committee in charge of each individual node commissioned the *créditos* from the committee that ran the network as a whole, the original Bernal node. This network commission kept a running tally on membership and was in charge of issuing the 50 *créditos*, called a "social franchise," to each new member. Beginning in 1999 problems arose within the General Barter Network, the *Red General del Trueque* (or RGT), regarding how the social franchise system functioned at the individual node level. Specifically, divergences had to do with who should issue the chits, how many should be issued, how they should be used, and which bookkeeping method should be used to keep track of the whole business. The result was a split in Buenos Aires, with the present-day *Club del Trueque Zona Oeste* establishing a separate network. A similar situation brought into existence an independent network, the *Red Nacional del Trueque*, in the province of Córdoba.

With the jump in the number of participants in 2002, the amount of social franchise chits circulating got out of control: counterfeiting and inflating the number of these chits was blamed for inflated prices in individual nodes. By mid-2002, 30 percent of the chits in circulation were said to be false; in October of the same year the RGT, the original network coordinating committee, indicated that, in fact, things were much worse: 90 percent of the *créditos* circulating in most nodes were false. Clearly, the system had collapsed; too many chits chasing too few goods and services offered for barter brought about a massive closing of nodes in the second half of 2002. In October 2002, according to the daily newspaper *Clarín*,[8] "People are abandoning barter: 40% of the clubs have closed."

Barter clubs were not immune to the 2001–2002 crisis that questioned the legitimacy of Argentine institutions in general. But before their eventual demise, they challenged members to re-create in some cases, or invent in others, a nonmonetary system for the exchange of goods and services. It is no accident that participants in this new social experience came to refer to themselves as *prosumers*.[9] Thanks to barter clubs, some people were able to resume productive activity that had been abandoned because of unemployment; others found an opportunity to exploit skills considered mere hobbies with no exchange value in the marketplace. The barter club phenomenon had no precedent in Argentina: never before had a space for consumption existed where impoverished middle-class members and structurally poor people interacted, each group trying to satisfy its particular needs. Paradoxically, in the case of the barter clubs, the same crisis that accentuated social segmentation gave rise to an organized activity that brought people together. In a country like Argentina, where the opportunity for social equality had formerly been public schools and universities, the fact that, in a context of crisis and need, a similar experience arose in the form of barter clubs is certainly worthy of note.

ORGANIZATIONS OF THE UNEMPLOYED

One of the most innovative responses to the effects of neoliberal policies has been the way the unemployed have organized and the kinds of activities they have carried out. Organizing for collective action on the part of the unemployed is highly unusual. This kind of movement has not developed in other countries with similar unemployment rates, no unemployment insurance, and a large informal economy. Similar movements have developed, however, in European countries with unemployment benefits.

The first step toward understanding the Argentine phenomenon is to examine two pilot experiences that occurred in the 1990s. In 1996 and 1997, respectively, in the southern province of Neuquén, the towns of Cutral-Co and Plaza Huincul rose up to protest the privatization of the government oil company, YPF. The term *piquetero* to designate protesting participants was born. Popular uprisings for the same reason also occurred from 1997 on in the towns of General Mosconi and Tartagal in the northwestern province of Salta.

That popular protest movements were set off by the privatizing of YPF at opposite ends of the country is no coincidence. This particular state enterprise had generated a "territorial civilizing model" that not only exploited a natural resource but also offered personnel an extensive network of social, recreational, and housing benefits, making it a veritable "state within a state" (Svampa and Pereyra 2003: 103).

Because YPF put into practice, as no other state enterprise did, the concept of state as social protector based on a model of social relations that combined social hierarchy with adequate pay and employment stability, it is not surprising that popular uprisings and roadblocks first appeared in company towns when YPF was privatized. In both places there was a strong communitarian component, which would also characterize the organizations of the unemployed to come. Of the different

responses to neoliberal policies analyzed here, it is in the organizations of the unemployed and reopened factories that the
Argentine trade union tradition is most evident.

As in other areas of the country where state-run enterprises
were dismantled in the 1990s, the social and economic
consequences of privatizing and restructuring YPF were devastating. When YPF withdrew from General Mosconi and Tartagal in
1993, oil pumping and drilling activity dropped 73 percent, and
there were 75 percent fewer jobs. In Cutral-Co and Plaza Huincul
in the south, a region less diversified than the northern province
of Salta, the drop in production was aggravated by the transfer
of YPF office personnel and workers to the provincial capital of
Neuquén. As a result, in May 2001, while unemployment was
running at 15.2 percent in the city of Neuquén and Greater
Neuquén, in Cutral-Co and Plaza Huincul, it was 32.5 percent.
By the same token, while unemployment in the city of Salta was
17.1 percent, in General Mosconi it was 42.8 percent.

In June 1996, in the two southern towns, a "multisectorial"
commission called on the population to block the national
highway after rejecting the provincial governor's decision to
suspend bidding. Twenty thousand demonstrators responded,
supported by local politicians. A permanent state of assembly was maintained at the roadblock, and a group of leaders
opposing local politicians soon appeared: when the first round
of negotiations with the governor was due to begin, *piqueteros*
refused to allow local party politicians to represent them at the
bargaining table. A few days later, the demonstrators decided
to maintain the roadblock in spite of the governor's decision
to use force to reopen the highway to transit.

In this first massive roadblock, and in a second one a year
later, it was the presence of a broad spectrum of social sectors,

including at times local political and business leaders, that kept the provincial government from using force to reopen the highway. The presence of the national mass media also played its part in forestalling indiscriminate repression.

According to Svampa and Pereyra (2003), the popular uprising that cut the highway in June 1996 gave rise to a demand for "historical reparation" for the communities devastated by the withdrawal of YPF. In fact, the highway was not reopened until a generous welfare package for the poor and the unemployed had been agreed on, along with a moratorium on evictions and bankruptcy proceedings. There was a cathartic component in these highway-cutting demonstrations, in the sense that they were an opportunity for giving voice to a diverse array of demands. Highway cutting soon became institutionalized as a method in which people came together to debate and air collective demands, making plain at the same time their extreme distrust of traditional means for mediating social conflict.

The popular uprisings in Neuquén brought to light not only the potential of this particular template for social action but also that the only possible response to the economic restructuring underway was to mobilize the entire community. Thus, it was that the *piquetero* (or road cutting) movement was born in places where a well-established way of life had been abruptly dismantled, with decollectivization affecting a wide social spectrum. The cradle of the *piquetero* movement is to be found in distant state oil company towns, and among the first *piqueteros* were formerly well-paid employees of the former welfare state. They enjoyed security, as had their families before them for generations, all having been socialized in an environment where stability and social welfare were traditions.

The other space where organizations of the unemployed developed and gained adherents were the popular neighborhoods in greater Buenos Aires, where the *piquetero* movement began with fits and starts. As unemployment began to spread in the early 1990s, grassroots organizations disappeared, and clientele-type relationships took their place. Working-class neighborhoods went from having a small minority of unemployed people to being neighborhoods where working people were the minority. At times as a result of clientele networks and at others through the efforts of autonomous organizations, common cooking pots, community meal centers, and snack centers for children sprang up. They demanded that the state provide food, bus passes for the unemployed, medicine, and the like.

Then one such organization in the greater Buenos Aires community of Florencio Varela decided to imitate the highway-cutting activity in distant provinces. Groups of unemployed people gathered together and blocked a highway, and the government responded with several hundred stipends for the unemployed. The success of this initial experience in Florencio Varela caused many small organizations of the unemployed to rapidly change their agenda, and the demand for social stipends soon became generalized. Not only were these stipends—originally instituted by Carlos Menem to subdue dissatisfaction in the provinces during his reelection campaign—extended in 1997 but they also had more and more organizations demanding them.[10]

The number of stipends obtained was usually less than what had originally been demanded, but the relative success of the road-blocking mobilizations attracted more and more unemployed men and women, and the demand for stipends grew. For its part the government constantly attempted to remove or disqualify stipend recipients by alleging irregularities. Maintaining beneficiaries on the roll meant that organizations had to designate people to lobby government offices and do paperwork, and new mobilizations demanded more stipends had to be organized.

Beneficiaries were required to provide a service in exchange for the stipend, which generally involved performing some task under the direction of the municipal government. As a result, organizations that were successful in getting stipends by blocking highways lost members when beneficiaries came under the control of the city officials who supervised the activities they carried out, often the same local politicians who had formerly belonged to the enemy camp. This led to the demand that the tasks required to receive the stipend be supervised by the organization of the unemployed. The result was a number of diverse kinds of productive and community activities—bakeries, concrete block production, dressmaking, house building, among others. Stipend-receiving members therefore remained within the organization, and new mobilizations could be organized to demand stipends for more unemployed persons. Over time, the *piquetero* organizations became, for all practical purposes, "labor unions for the unemployed."

In a strange way, two key elements present in any urban environment were brought together by the *piqueteros:* neighborhoods and transit. Unlike the urban model in the United States, in Buenos Aires suburbs have traditionally been home to the less well-off sectors of society. Sociospatial segregation increased in the 1990s, with poverty becoming increasingly concentrated in the neighborhoods farthest from the city center. Unable to pay bus or train fare, the unemployed were relegated to remaining in their neighborhood. Segregation was economic, and the unemployed naturally gathered together in each neighborhood.

Given these circumstances, the obvious way to protest for those out of work and unable to leave their neighborhood was for them to block traffic on highways and major thoroughfares to stop—to the degree possible—urban life from going on without them. As organizations for the unemployed grew and efforts among different neighborhood groups were coordinated, it became possible to contemplate obstructing traffic across the urban frontier par excellence: the bridges that join the city with greater Buenos Aires. In the southern part of the city, these bridges cross the Riachuelo River. The first part of the city to be industrialized, the southern sector contains the oldest working-class neighborhoods. Full of shuttered factories at the present time, it currently is home to a high percentage of the long-term unemployed and people living in poverty.

It is along the frontiers of all kinds separating sectors within a city that social protest takes place. The setting for the ongoing struggle between the unemployed and the powers that be is the bridges; by closing them down, the *piqueteros* have put into practice the idea of laying siege to the city of Buenos Aires. As can be seen in Figure 5.1, highway cutting peaked in 2002. The Pueyrredón Bridge, the main viaduct in the southern part of the city, became a key location for *piquetero* roadblocks. It was on this bridge that two *piqueteros* were slain when police attacked protesters on June 26, 2002. Public repudiation of these killings was so strong that interim president Eduardo Duhalde was obliged to leave office six months earlier than anticipated.

Historically speaking, neighborhood organizations have handled reproduction-related demands (housing issues, for

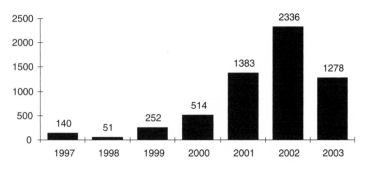

EVOLUTION OF ROAD BLOCK
(1997-2003)

Source: Centro de Estudios Nueva Mayoría

Figure 5.1

example), whereas labor unions have been in charge of distribution demands linked to production. With the onset of mass unemployment, the rationale underpinning this division of labor was no longer feasible: the lack of jobs has become a reproductive issue, and the demands of those out of work have been taken up by the territorial organizations of the unemployed themselves, not by labor unions. Mass unemployment not only is responsible for territorial segregation but also explains why the demand for jobs or unemployment stipends has been led by territorial organizations, as well as why the traditional gender division of labor has broken down. The former structuring that lined up reproduction, territory, and women on one side and production, jobs, the public sphere, and men on the other did not survive the 1990s.

At the present time, organizations of the unemployed do much more than protest against the lack of jobs: they distribute thousands of unemployment stipends and food packages received from the national government; they organize and run community meal centers; and some organizations run production activities that include making baked goods, clothes, cement blocks, and even houses, among other things. Poorly nourished and with inadequate health care and educational opportunities, *piquetero* group members lead precarious lives. Unlike other poor people, however, they do have access to food and receive tutoring for their school-age children, as well as receive medicine and other benefits from time to time, thanks to the existence of the social solidarity network that has come into being.

The spectrum of organizations of the unemployed is ideologically and politically heterogeneous. Some groups support the current government, whereas other groups strongly oppose it. Certain sectors have their roots in traditional left-wing organizations, whereas others aspire to autonomy and find their inspiration in the self-management movement.

Any evaluation of the *piquetero* movement must be partial. Although it is undoubtedly one of the richest political experiences in present-day Argentina, it is also true that *piquetero* organizations have been losing social support since 2004. Among the many reasons for this are the following: economic revitalization has raised the expectations of the Argentine middle class, and the policy of criminalizing people blocking transit and trying perpetrators in a court of law has had some success.

Certainly one important factor was the change that took place in the location and time chosen for *piquetero* protest, and the subsequent change in its meaning. Beginning in late 2003, the setting moved from the urban frontier in general and its bridges in particular to downtown, especially the

Plaza de Mayo (the traditional site for protest in Argentina), as well as other major city center thoroughfares. However, these demonstrations and roadblocks no longer interrupted the daily commuter routine of a society that was reluctant to assume mass unemployment as one of the consequences of neoliberal policies in the 1990s. Mobilizations became less dramatic and more routine, a sign that what had begun in the late 1990s as a national protest movement questioning the viability of a way of life that excluded so many people was increasingly being viewed as a sectorial protest.

WORKER TAKEOVERS

The unemployed and their families are not the only ones affected by mass unemployment. When almost half the economically active population of any country is out of a job, the remaining people are constantly afraid of losing theirs, an ideal situation for instituting "job flexibilization" norms and increasing discipline in the workplace. Naturally enough, the fear of not finding anther job is particularly acute when a factory closes its doors for one reason or another. It was in this context that a new form of collective action arose in Argentina: worker takeovers to keep factory doors open.

The first takeovers date from the late 1990s, although the large majority occurred in 2001 to 2002. The protagonists are usually workers facing the real or highly likely possibility of their factory closing down, either because its owners have decided to gut it or because it has gone bankrupt. Metalworking concerns lead the list of reopened factories, followed by food processing and textile plants, printing presses, and slaughterhouses, among others (see Fajn 2003; Lavaca 2005; Palomino 2003; Rebón 2004).

Takeover processes vary widely. They usually begin with broken contracts—wages are reduced, then not paid or paid with IOUs, social security payments are not made, followed by dismissals and layoffs. Some firms try to reach an agreement with creditors, others begin bankruptcy proceedings, and still others simply close down. Damián Giordano, a factory administrator, described the situation as follows:

> During the past decade we have seen factories and other enterprises systematically destroyed, almost as if they were the military objectives of an invading army. It seemed, and seems, like a naval battle: hit and sunk; hit and sunk … there was no way for us workers to respond to this kind of scenario. We were the passive observers of our own labor and social demise. Traditional mechanisms—work stoppage, strike—didn't work because there was no one to make demands to: the boss had disappeared and the state didn't, and still doesn't, have a response. Labor unions didn't have an answer either. (*La Nación* magazine, August 2002)

By 2004 more than 150 enterprises were being run by their workers; approximately half of them had been taken over by their employees; in other cases employees had simply stayed on and kept working after their employers left. For example, Celia Martínez, a worker at the Brukman textile factory, tells how the company began by not paying full wages, then reducing week by week what they paid until it covered only bus fare.

> "The last Friday before December 18 (2001), they gave us two pesos. We should have begun work on Monday and we said no. We had decided not to work Mondays in December to save on

bus fare. So we came on Tuesday. And Tuesday they said no, come back on Wednesday when it's surer we will have money. And we began to think they could fire us for abandoning the workplace. So we decided to fight. We came to work on Tuesday and began that day at 10 in the morning to fight for more money, at least 50 or 100 pesos. So we argued a lot with the boss.

When 2 PM came and we went downstairs, everybody was gone. So we decided to wait, thinking they had gone to get money and would be back. And we waited, and now we are still waiting ..." she said ironically. No plan was followed in the takeover of the Brukman factory. The employees simply remained inside waiting for the bosses to return with the money owed them. According to Celia, "it was by accident. Many people stayed on because they didn't have bus fare to go home. I stayed until around 10 PM and then came back. I was there at 6 AM the next day, but my *compañeros* had stayed on and are still staying on.[11]

In other cases, workers decided to collectively occupy a shuttered factory. This is what happened at the Forja metal-working plant, where workers fought for more than a year to get a difficult-to-obtain loan and get the machinery operating again. When security guards appeared with orders to evict the workers, the workers responded that they had not invaded the premises—which would be criminally punishable as usurpation—but had instead remained in their workplace, protecting the plant, the machinery it held, their own job security and income with which to support their families. In this instance the constitutional right to work and legally earn a livelihood was vindicated.

Efforts were made to construct a juridical framework to provide temporary protection for employees attempting to make operable and run places of work that had been closed down by their owners. As a general rule, work cooperatives were established, although there were cases in which the enterprise's legal structure remained unchanged, and others in which workers became shareholders. At times the juridical framework adopted responded to workers' ideological orientation; in others, it was dictated by the need to keep credit lines open or simply by the requirements of doing business in the formal economy.

In general, the decision to form a work cooperative is made by the workers following a period of discussion among those involved. The term "new work cooperatives" is often used to emphasize the collective nature of this new way of forming associations, as well as the solidarity networks that sustain them.

The question of differentiated wage scales and workplace norms are the subject of heated debate among workers. In many new work cooperatives, employees all earn the same wage, regardless of the position occupied, and days off vary according to output. In other reopened factories a differential wage scale is adopted to keep specialists from taking better-paid jobs at other companies. In a minority of reopened firms, wages are tied to output or number of hours worked.

In the new work cooperatives, decisions are usually made collectively during a general assembly, in part because of the enterprise's structure and in part as a result of the experience of working as a group built up during the takeover process. One characteristic contributing to group solidarity is the fact that when problems arise or demand drops, working hours are reduced but nobody is let go. In spite of the limited amount of operating capital at their disposition, these cooperatives tend not to go into debt or seek loans. In short, workers who have opted for self-management to avoid unemployment confront the challenge of exploring the entire gamut of tools available within the framework of a cooperative enterprise.

The institutional context and political and cultural climate following December 2001 favored the growth of self-managed enterprises. The context also fostered relationships among them and other social movements such as the *piquetero* organizations and neighborhood general assemblies. Political parties, congressional representatives, government authorities, and even trade unions have also given them symbolic and material support; for example, donating food and standing with workers when the police threaten to evict them from the occupied factories.

Active solidarity—both for fostering group survival in the beginning and for making enterprises operable—keep cooperative enterprises that have successfully navigated these same stages. Umbrella organizations of reopened enterprises have supplied technical and legal expertise to self-managed businesses in trouble. The largest of the former is the National Movement of Recovered Enterprises (MNER). For example, one MNER member made a long-term loan available to a recently taken-over enterprise, permitting it to reestablish electricity and telephone service. Different self-management networks also worked to gain passage of Law #5708 in the province of Buenos Aires, which permits the expropriation of real estate that can then be assigned to workers as a permanent loan or as a donation. There are also cases of self-managed enterprises that have obtained economic support and other donations from the state.

When compared with the number of factories that have shut down during this period, the number of self-managed enterprises is small. But still, the movement's significance lies in the fact that one more way of imagining activities to mitigate the effects of deindustrialization and certain kinds of business practices has been put into practice.

OTHER ISSUES AND MOVEMENTS

The principal organizations that grew up in Argentina as a response to neoliberal reform clearly show that Argentines did not passively succumb to its social consequences, as was alleged early on. Rounding out social activity in recent years have been popular assemblies in the city of Buenos Aires, along with organizations advocating justice, security, equality, and the right to be different.

On December 19, 2001, when President Fernando de la Rúa declared a state of siege to repress supermarket sacking and protest demonstrations, middle-class sectors in the city of Buenos Aires responded with a *cacerolazo,* the beating of pots and pans, their first mass protest in years. We single out for special attention two of the many significant aspects of those tumultuous days. The first is the novel relationship between private space and public space: the *cacerolazo* began with people grabbing a pot or pan and standing out on their balcony to beat it. More and more people joined in. This was a public protest, the scenarios of which were living rooms, street doors, or patios of private apartment buildings and houses. The resulting din gave eloquent expression to the tensions of the epoch. Middle-class sectors, whose tendency had been to withdraw from public spaces in the interest of security and socialize in private, reemerged as a force in public space.

The transition was visible: people took to the street at 11 p.m. or 12 a.m. to protest. They came in nightclothes or shorts, wearing slippers or flip-flops; some were barefooted. Nobody spoke, yet everybody made noise to express the strong feeling of rejection they shared.

Shortly afterward these same social actors began holding assemblies open to all in Buenos Aires neighborhoods. By mid-January 2002, neighborhood assemblies were being held all around the city of Buenos Aires, in some parts of greater Buenos Aires, and in a number of provincial cities. As Svampa (2005) affirmed, neighborhood assemblies became a place for deliberating and organizing that broke with traditional political representation; here new forms of social self-organization stressing horizontality and favoring direct action came into being. Second, the assemblies signaled the emergence of a disruptive, sociopolitical protagonism that put an abrupt end to the fatalistic ideological discourse that had characterized the 1990s, making participants feel they had a concrete part to play in public life once again. And third, these new experiences placed middle-class sectors, especially in the city of Buenos Aires, center stage in Argentine political life once again.

In fact, neighborhood assemblies were a place where middle-class sectors reconstituted their political identity. They were attended by businessmen, civil servants, doctors, lawyers, teachers, and administrative employees, among others. Many participants were newly impoverished, and some suffered job insecurity. Out-of-work people of all kinds also attended, as did radicalized young people, many of whom made their political debut during assembly meetings. The assemblies were an open space for political debate on almost any subject where the underlying tension of whether democracy should be direct or delegated—the very question that had given birth to the assemblies—was never far from the surface. The experience, however, was short-lived. Once the economic and political situation showed signs of stabilizing, the assemblies disbanded, frequently victims of disputes between groups with divergent agendas and inexperienced in political debate. In some cases participants moved on to more practical community projects with specific goals.

As crisis conditions became less acute, another movement arose in response to the other great fear, the one that followed on those of unemployment and job insecurity: urban insecurity. The crime rate increased during the 1990s in almost the entire region, accompanied by frequent examples of the illegal use of power on the part of the police. It is impossible to avoid relating the increase in the crime rate to the social consequences of neoliberal reform. By the same token, the different facets of urban insecurity are also an issue of great importance in public opinion, giving rise to diverse, often contradictory, responses over the years. One response has been the protests against police violence. Since the return of democracy, institutional violence has become one of the main spheres of action of human rights organizations in Argentina, occupying a prominent place in public opinion in the 1990s.

Present-day protests against institutional violence are seen as the continuation of the human rights movement that opposed state terrorism, disappearances, and torture during the 1976–83 military dictatorship. Because human rights networks and organizations were based outside Argentina during the dictatorship, protests against institutional violence once democracy returned have had an international dimension. At the same time, after details of the regional repressive effort known as the Condor Operation (see chapter 1) became known, attempts to find children of the disappeared who were given up for secret adoption have increased. The case of the reunion of the Argentine poet Juan Gelman with his grand-daughter in Uruguay, which occurred thanks to international pressure, is a case in point. Another was the arrest of the Chilean dictator Augusto Pinochet in London, the impact of which was regional.

In the 1990s protests opposing illegal police violence against young victims who had committed no crime (or whose crimes were not discouraged by the police) were common. The protests against these local crimes gave rise to movements organized by the parents, usually the mothers—the Mother of Pain—of these victims. Over time these protests have also become institutional-ized. Centro de Estudios Legales y Sociales (CELS) created in 1979 and Comisión contra la Represión policial (CORREPI) are two organizations whose objective is to denounce police repression and demand justice when police violence has been proved.

A second variation has been the demonstrations demand-ing greater urban security that have been organized not only in Buenos Aires but also in other Latin American cities such as Mexico City, Asunción, and Santo Domingo. A paradig-matic case has been the demand for greater security led by Juan Carlos Blumberg, the father of an upper-middle-class student and only child who was kidnapped and then killed in Buenos Aires in 2004 in a case that moved the entire country. The marches organized by the dead youth's father resulted in the largest demonstrations in Argentina in recent years. Blumberg's demands include stiffer criminal sentences and an end to police corruption. Although association with antidemocratic personages has aroused suspicions regarding

Blumberg's intentions, what interests us here is how his call to protest, which crystallized latent demands largely ignored by the powers that be in the region, was massively responded to by the public at large.

Another demand for justice centers around two anti-Semitic terrorist attacks, the most serious in Argentine history, the first of which destroyed the Israeli embassy in Buenos Aires in 1992, and the second, the AMIA (Argentine Israelite Mutual Association) building in 1994, causing more than one hundred deaths. Relatives of the dead have spearheaded the demand for justice, forming organizations such as "Active Memory," which seeks to keep the memory of the attack alive and bring the perpetrators before a court of law. Argentine law enforcement forces are implicated in both terrorist attacks.

Clearly, human rights tied to ethnicity had become a key campaign in the 1990s. We discussed the relevance of ethnic issues in chapter 4, as well as the large number of organizations developed around gender issues in these same years. In 2003 around 180 women's organizations were officially recognized, 33 of which were dedicated to family planning (Faur 2005). Other topics that groups organized around were equality for women, reproductive health, and the prevention of domestic violence, and advances have been made in a number of areas. For example, domestic violence is now considered a social problem by the state, which has developed specific policies and programs to deal with it. Sexual minority rights have also gained ground: homosexual groups succeeded in getting a law of civil union passed by the city government in Buenos Aires, which is among the most advanced in the world. As in other parts of the world, gender issues arouse strong passions and opposition in Argentina; a number of organizations supported by the Catholic Church work actively to prevent any liberalization in the sexual and reproductive health laws already on the books, and other conservative institutions have joined in to oppose birth control and abortion, the latter still a political taboo even though between 400,000 and 500,000 abortions are performed annually in Argentina.

A look back over the ground covered in this chapter suggests three general conclusions that challenge certain consensus views built up over the past decade. In the first place, far from being a period during which Argentine society passively bore the consequences of neoliberal reform, Argentina developed ways not only to resist but also to reconstruct collectively when resistance failed (when state enterprises were privatized, for example). Of course collective action in these years was nothing like the classic working-class mobilizations of earlier times, and the social movements that rose up did not follow the dynamic of mass mobilization evident in the 1980s. Especially in the beginning, reactions were scattered and disjointed. Perhaps this is why the period was prematurely diagnosed as one of inaction on the part of popular sectors. In hindsight these fragmented reactions appear as the heterogeneous seeds of new forms of action, opposition, and recomposition corresponding to the demands of the times and therefore very different from the forms collective action had taken in the recent past.

Second, this heterogeneity questions one of the key concepts of "new social question" theory in Europe (Touraine 1991; Rosanvallon 1995). As unemployment spread, it appears to have marked a transition from redistribution demands to a period in which social conflict centered around exclusion. Both kinds of conflicts took place during the 1990s, both lending themselves perfectly to collective action. Clearly, the struggles to keep the workplace open and to support the unemployed—factory takeovers, the *piquetero* movement—are the requisite first steps to avoid exclusion. And once this first stage has been successfully completed, protagonists are in a position to question how the fruits of their labor are distributed. A case in point is the discussions on wage scales that took place in reopened factories. Far from ruling out demands for redistribution, the new ways of organizing for public protest and interacting with other social actors pave the way for making them possible.

And finally, social action in the 1990s illustrates the relationship existing between movements organized around specific demands (in the Argentine case social demands) and other kinds of rights—in other words, what has been termed "the indivisibility of rights." In fact, just as Argentine society did not passively accept the consequences of neoliberal reform, in other areas of social life, more or less directly related to these same consequences, collective action proliferated during this period. In many cases, the goal sought—more or less successfully—was interaction among groups organized around different kinds of civil, social, and political rights. For example, feminist groups collaborated with the *piqueteros* to help the latter incorporate gender concerns into their practices; neighborhood assemblies attempted to work with communal meal centers; and in the aftermath of the 2001–2002 crisis, different groups of performing artists established contact with neighborhood assemblies and reopened factories and *piquetero* organizations. This should in no way be taken to mean that an idyllic period of cooperation and respect for the rights of others had begun: not only were intragroup initiatives often fragmentary and short-lived, many were co-opted by the powers that be, and others simply failed. It should be noted that not all collective action was democratically inspired and sought to extend social and individual rights. In the recent demonstrations protesting urban insecurity, for example, some of the demands, if granted, would violate individual rights and very likely accentuate existing divisions and mistrust between social sectors.

In sum, different sectors of Argentine society have acted, and will continue to act, in different ways in response to the new social, political, and cultural reality they face, and any simplification of this complex panorama should be rejected out of hand. An example was the vision of Argentina as paradigm of the mobilization against neoliberalism and repudiation of globalization that circulated widely a few years back, which was just as false as the vision of Argentina as the IMF poster child that preceded it. As a matter of fact, the spectacular failure of the latter should give pause to any further model making regarding the former "breadbasket of the world." What we have attempted to do in the course of the preceding pages is show how, within a specific historical context, Argentines sought in their own prior experience the tools with which to intervene more or less effectively in public life. Our fervent wish is that this social capital lay the foundation for an ever-more democratic and egalitarian future for the country and its citizenry.

Some Reflections in Closing

The Argentina case opens up questions regarding a number of political and theoretical commonplaces on the effects of neo-liberalism as well as certain mechanistic views of globalization. On the conceptual plane, but with strong political implications, one often hears that states and nations are disappearing; that globalization is making territorial questions and sovereignty claims irrelevant; that the foregoing inevitably affects economic policy and the job market; that national frontiers and identities are being erased; and that the above is an unavoidable process that, in the end, will benefit the vast majority of people, who in the meantime must learn new ways to exercise their civil rights and refrain from anachronistic forms of protest like street demonstrations. In Argentina each of the above points has proved to be only partially true. The error is to treat these partial truths as if they were transcendental, absolute ones, applying them indis-criminately and turning specific, contingent roads to develop-ment into the only way for a country and its people to progress.

THE STATE IS NOT A VANISHING SPECIES

It is true (and not for the first time) that the ability for indepen-dent action on the part of any given country has been weakened by external contingencies. But different countries have reacted in different ways to this situation. For example, the same neo-liberal reform policies whose extreme versions were applied in Argentina were applied differently in others. Two cases in point are the way privatization was handled in Uruguay and the rules and regulations governing speculative financial capitals in Chile. There could have been modifications in the application of the model in Argentina too, but there were not. In fact, we can conclude that the least desirable variation is the one that denies contingencies and affirms it is "the only way." And any pretense of silencing dissent to avoid conflict implies reducing the political imagination of the country involved.

All around the world the state is withdrawing from the institutional role of providing for economic development, income redistribution, and social welfare. The process has been heterogeneous, and the margin for negotiation uneven, with the policy template being applied case by case. But, in spite of this diversity, neoliberalism has been quite successful in destroying local versions of the "welfare state." However, this historical tendency can be turned around or transformed. It is important to stress this point, because according to the new teleology, it is precisely this tendency that proves that the state no longer fills the role of main social articulator and key hegemonic agent.

It is also important to distinguish between the social and the repressive functions of the state. Because although it is true that in many countries the state no longer protects or provides social security for those in need, it is also true that the power to limit and repress social movements has remained intact. Security and armed forces are still in place in most countries, and in many their numbers have increased. In the social and political crises that the reduced social role of the state provoked, its repressive power has proved to be very strong.

In the second place, the Argentine case exemplifies the selective withdrawal of a state that reduces certain functions while strengthening others. The clearest example is the freezing of bank deposits, or *corralito,* in Argentina in 2001. A state that can confiscate the savings of an entire nation wields a degree of power easy to overlook in developed countries with stronger states. The Argentine state also expanded its territorial presence with welfare policies applied for the first time ever. Above and beyond the insufficiency of these policies to even begin to compensate for the social degradation that has occurred, their existence is evidence of a change in the type of regulation carried out by the state and in the nature of the social actor itself rather than of the state's withdrawal or disappearance.

In other words, the state as institution that exercises territorial sovereignty has not disappeared and won't any time soon. There has been a dramatic change, however, in the way the state articulates its diverse functions. Indeed, the loss of the "central state" model (Cavarozzi 1999) implies not the end of the state but rather the state's fragmentation into a series of ministates that act more or less efficiently, employing different tools and mechanisms, according to the region, the area of competence, and the particular juncture being dealt with.

NATIONS ARE NOT A VANISHING SPECIES

In Latin American history, neither nations nor nationalism preceded the state. The "nationality principle" came long after independence. State land was distributed according to norms employed by colonial administrators, and later on it was determined by the power struggle between city and hinterland in the absence of any community identity. In this sense the nation as stimulus for images of belonging to a community came after the formation of the state, whose institutions and civil rights and cultural policies performed the hard work of nationalization.

As the nation was the product of the state, and a state that expels citizens does not produce nations, it might be supposed the nation is a vanishing species. This is not the case, however, for at least two reasons. In the first place, no other interlocutor has arisen with the same degree of legitimacy and legal power to define civil rights. So although social movements protest against transnational organizations, these organizations do not have the juridical policy-making power to respond if they wanted to. In general, social movements demand that the state assume a certain position with regard to organizations or institutions. For example, in Argentina no social mobilization makes demands of the International Monetary Fund, the United Nations, or Mercosur. The demands that are formulated, however, direct the Argentine state to take such and such a position vis-à-vis the International Monetary Fund, the United Nations, or Mercosur member countries.

And second, in some of these processes, national identification has played a pertinent part in articulating demands on the state. In the face of increasing social exclusion, belonging to a nation can become at times—together with humanitarian motives—a powerful argument in favor of coming to the aid of a person or group. Waving Argentine flags, teachers struck for higher wages in the 1990s, and workers for the national airline, Aerolíneas Argentinas, made use of national symbols in their fight against its sale to the Spanish state. These same national symbols appeared in *piquetero* roadblocks, neighborhood assemblies, and other protest movements. At certain junctures, less state—in its welfare-providing capacity—can mean more nation. And, in the broad sense of the term, a collective sense of belonging can also mean more nationalism.

In light of all this, the quite extensively held belief that nationalism is found exclusively in the soccer stadium does not stand up under examination.

A RESURGENCE OF "OLD" SOCIOPOLITICAL IDENTIFICATIONS AND STREET DEMONSTRATIONS ARE BACK

Ethnic identifications have taken on new relevance in Argentina, a tendency that often implies demands so specific that fragmentation ensues. Both policies recognizing diversity and new forms of xenophobia have grown in importance since the 1990s.

Class identification has acquired new political power. A statement repeated again and again in recent decades was that class identifications had been set aside in the new social movements. Nevertheless, in the most impoverished neighborhoods, "unemployed workers" organized to demand from the state jobs and job-creating policies. So one of the most visible and relevant forms popular organizing has taken in recent years is class oriented. Broad sectors of society have mobilized around issues as diverse as political representation, social rights, and insecurity, among many others. In the mid-1990s terms such as *demobilization* and *defeat* were used to describe the social situation. But in hindsight it is evident that demobilization was followed by recomposition, and new ways of organizing appeared on the scene. Innovations in ways of mobilizing do not necessarily mean that an old issue like distribution has been replaced by a new one, exclusion. The Argentine experience shows that the two issues are intertwined. As soon as a little bit of inclusion is achieved, distributive conflicts begin taking place. It could not be otherwise in a context like the Latin American one where low wages and contingent jobs mean working does not necessarily guarantee inclusion, because 75 percent of the salaried workers is poor in the region (Hoffman and Centeno 2003). Indeed, at the time we are writing this book—December 2004—many unions are demanding higher wages by means of collective action.

What happened in Argentina has shown neoliberal promises to be false, the most important of which was, of course, the trickle down effect, according to which economic growth in and of itself trickles down to benefit all social sectors. This being the case, income concentration at the top should not be checked, because that is the sector with the most human capital and the greatest capacity for saving and, supposedly, productive investment. And these factors will generate growth, which will then spill over and benefit society as a whole. This did not happen, not only in Argentina and many other Latin American countries but in other parts of the world as well. During the 1990s there were periods of economic expansion when the GNP grew, but this didn't prevent unemployment, poverty, and social inequality from increasing just the same. As the Argentine case clearly shows, economic growth alone, in the absence of job creation and income distribution policies, does not benefit the society as a whole.

According to a second axiom in the neoliberal creed, flexibilizing a rigid job market will reduce labor costs. This, in turn, will increase jobs in the formal economy and decrease those in the informal one. This was the rationale for passing labor flexibility laws in Argentina. But this promise, too, went unfulfilled: in Argentina the more the job market was flexibilized, the greater was the number of people working off the books, with no increase in employment in the formal economy. When queried on the subject, the neoliberals responded that flexibilization had been insufficient, and more was needed. This led to a new round of flexibility legislation, which only made matters worse.

In the third place, globalization cheerleaders affirmed that the growing participation of third world countries in the world market would improve the wages paid unskilled workers. The reason given was that rising demand for primary products on the part of central countries would increase the demand for the unskilled workers that produced them, whose wages would rise. Thus the spread would be reduced between skilled and unskilled workers' wages. This also didn't happen in Argentina or in almost all the rest of Latin America, where the gap between the income of the skilled and the unskilled continued growing as globalization spread in the 1990s.

Fourth, by increasing the educational level of the population in general and low-income sectors in particular, globalization was said to help reduce income disparity. The supposition was that a more equitable distribution of human capital, meaning more individuals with diplomas on the job market, would reduce the spread between skilled and unskilled sectors. Although few people would deny the benefits of making education more widely available, neoliberal ideologues went further, alleging that an increase in the availability of basic education would, in itself, generate a more equitable salary spread. The Argentine experience has shown that this clearly was not the case. In fact, higher educational levels during the 1980s and 1990s not only didn't reduce income inequality but reached new highs during this period of time.

And finally, predictions regarding the effectiveness of the "poverty-fighting" policies that would accompany neoliberal reform were wrong. In theory, the solution for the "social cost"—read increase in poverty—generated by neoliberal reform focused policies that would help lift well-chosen target groups out of poverty. More than a decade of different types of focused projects has shown that they do help mitigate poverty while in effect but have no lasting effect on poverty levels, and thus do nothing to eradicate poverty.

The Argentine case is an example of how the neoliberal narrative postulates a particular, extremely rigid, relationship among the economic, the political, and the social dimensions. The job of politics is to guarantee that the economy functions with the least number of fetters and conditioning factors possible, while social policy should deal with individuals excluded from the working world (Rosanvallon 1995). The legitimacy of the neoliberal creed in Argentina rested on a series of powerful metaphors and beliefs, reinforced by recent traumatic experiences. Indeed, the idea that "everything has a cost" is a universally accepted legal principal; what was not debated in Argentina was who should pay it. In addition, the fantasy of joining the first world became crystallized in the peso–dollar equivalency, which put Buenos Aires on a superficially equal footing with European capitals and the United States. What was omitted was any serious discussion of what would happen when the overvalued currency bubble inevitably burst.

The rise and fall of the neoliberal narrative brings to mind the grammar used to construct sociopolitical tales. A "societal paradigm" is constructed: establish a diagnosis that, like any diagnosis, includes a desirable type of solution. And the more it appears as the only possible alternative, the greater its power of persuasion and legitimacy will be. One important detail to keep in mind is that the 1990s were the first time liberalism had enjoyed grassroots legitimacy in Argentina. Prior to the 1990s it had always been an elitist, minority movement that opposed Peronism, allying itself with military dictatorships from the 1960s on to compensate for its lack of popularity. This time it was different: a special narrative was constructed. No sectorial enemy equivalent to the category of "oligarchy" during the first Peronist period, or of "subversion" during the dictatorship, was identified. In the absence of a sharply defined "other"—internal or external—as enemy, stability became the single common good, finally permitting the reconciliation of state and society, individual and community, in Argentina. But like all paradigms, and unlike myths that are impervious to reality, the neoliberal construct finally succumbed under the cumulative weight of a series of events, receiving its coup de grâce in December 2001.

During the neoliberal period, other mirror games were created among Southern Cone countries, with some old rivalries reappearing and others fading away. Bolivian and Paraguayans, the poor neighbors, came to be seen as part of a "migratory flood," unlike anything seen for decades, inundating Argentina in search of the first world salaries it paid, thanks to the peso–dollar parity. Chile, the formerly poor neighbor who had faced off against Argentina in a number of border conflicts, changed its image: when Chile turned out to be a better student than Argentina when it came to successfully applying neoliberal policies, its economic performance and global significance caused envy and a certain misgiving among Argentines. In addition, formerly viewed as a potentially dangerous, transborder "invader," Brazil became a mirror for the worst fears of the Argentine middle class: "a country of rich and poor, with nothing in between." Also, thanks to the implementation of Mercosur, Brazil became both desirable as a market and unfair competition for Argentine industry because it paid lower salaries. And then there is

Uruguay. With less inequality and better protection from the devastating effects of neoliberal reform, when viewed from the other bank of the Río de la Plata, it awakens fond nostalgia in Argentines as a somewhat bucolic, albeit lethargic, version of Argentina, or rather the Río de la Plata region, in the old days.

To be comprehensive, of course, any evaluation of the 1990s should include a series of nuances and complex areas. No period is monochromatic, and many academicians and intellectuals point to positive changes such as the following: technological updating in agriculture and some industrial sectors; the benefits of increased access to the global marketplace for Argentine exports; greater intercultural contact with cosmopolitan implications; and along the same lines, increased contact with the world and democratic voices on subjects such as gender, environment, and ethnic and sexual diversity. A debate on and evaluation of nuances is pending. We must add, however, that there are no nuances surrounding general tendencies of the period like the jumps in deindustrialization, inequality, and job contingency.

Be that as it may, at this time we can pose two questions regarding Argentina. The first, the depth of the neoliberal reform carried out on one hand and the lack of a profound sociocultural reaction on the other, leads us to question the myth of the existence of an egalitarian Argentina in the past, a myth that the authors, in part, adhere to. Was this really the case? The strong upward mobility of the migrant generations was real. Neither national origin nor religious belief posed an obstacle to gaining diplomas and going into business. But does that add up to an egalitarian society? Or is it not, instead, that when upward mobility was feasible for many people, it did not matter who was beside you? If the latter is true, then egalitarian standards were not internalized in Argentina as they apparently were in Uruguay, where neoliberal reform attempts were resisted by broad sectors of the society during the 1990s. If egalitarianism had become an integral part of the national culture in Argentina, possibly the social reaction to neoliberal reform—independent of those directly affected by it—would have been more visible.

And finally, we are witnessing the construction of a new narrative, which could be termed post-neoliberal. Post-neoliberal not because the economic and social consequences of neoliberal policies have been overcome—quite the contrary, they are in plain sight—and not because a new national narrative or way of fitting into the world at large has appeared. It is post-neoliberal because neoliberalism in Argentina in particular, and in the Southern Cone in general, no longer has the weight that being the "only way" lent it for so long, with the capacity to establish the bounds within which the socio-political imagination functioned. Post-neoliberal also because collective action and changes in political imagery now suggest a reaction to the negative effects of neoliberalism. Perhaps the best description is that it is a transitional narrative arising out of the fissures in its predecessor as reaction first, and then recomposition. This is why we use the term *post-neoliberal* instead of choosing an entirely new name.

The post-neoliberal narrative refers, explicitly and implicitly, to neoliberalism and, at the same time, repositions subjects such as distribution or the situation of the privileged that were veiled before. It also establishes a new relationship with ideas on nationhood in Latin America. This is not to say that theory is being put into practice or is any value judgment on the acts of post-neoliberal governments intended. What is clear is that we are in the presence of a new narrative corresponding to a new period of time, characterized by similarities and differences with neoliberalism, but that will undoubtedly lead us to see Argentina and its surroundings in a new light.

INTRODUCTION

1. In the first pages of *Facundo*, Sarmiento (1977) said, "The evil afflicting the Argentine Republic is its extension, the desert that surrounds it on all sides, that advances in its entrails." For his part, Alberdi (1915) indicates in his *Bases*, "But what is the Constitution best suited to a desert? The one that serves to make it disappear. ... So this should be the political objective, and it can be no other. ... Thus, in America to govern is to settle."

CHAPTER 1

1. A significant amount of what is known abut Operation Condor came from "the Terror Archives," documents found in Paraguay related to the detention and disappearance of Paraguayans in which the coordination of repressive forces is described.
2. Obviously what is meant by "welfare" and "integration" in the Southern Cone must be examined. In this regard, see Grimson (2000a).
3. See Wilson (2000).

CHAPTER 2

1. Between 1976 and 1989 the gross national product decreased to an average annual rate of 1.4 percent. From 1974 to 1990 the gross industrial product dropped 25 percent, industrial employment fell 40 percent, and the percentage of wages as part of national income decreased from 45 percent to 32 percent (Bayón and Saraví 2002).
2. In our analysis of the network of recently impoverished people we found that two products did not figure on their list of requests—food and clothing—not because they didn't need them but because of their highly charged symbolic significance as a sign of social destitution.

3. Ministerio de Salud y Acción Social, PAN, May 1984, Hintze op cit., p. 39, italicized by the present authors.

4. The analysis on hyperinflation is based in large part on the research carried out with S. Sigal (Sigal and Kessler 1997) and with V. Armony (Armony and Kessler 2004a, 2004b).

5. Somewhat arbitrarily characterized by us as more than 20 percent a month.

6. According to CEPAL (Economic Commission for Latin America) figures, retail prices increased 4,933 percent in 1989 and 1,343 percent in 1990; in Bolivia the corresponding figure was 8,170 percent in 1985, and in Peru it was 8,300 percent in 1990.

CHAPTER 3

1. The concept being referred to is Schutz's stock of knowledge. This author states that "any interpretation of the world is based on a reserve of prior experience, either our own or that of those who went before that have been transmitted by our parents and teachers; This experience, in the form of 'disposable knowledge' functions as reference schemes" (1987, 12). Cefai (1994, 112) referred to situations in which this reserve of experience doesn't provide elements for interpreting a new situation: "The problem arises when an actor doesn't know what to say or do, isn't able to understand what is happening, doesn't manage to understand or agree with other people, fails in his attempt to give a name to the structures for belonging used up to that time. ... He feels his 'comprehension structure' to be inadequate: his field of interpretative and motivational anticipation is inappropriate for defining and controlling the situation he is confronting."

2. Data on and tendencies for the case in Chile have been taken from Wormald, Cereceda, and Ugalde (2002).

3. Data on and tendencies for the case in Uruguay have been taken from Filgueira (2002) and Kessler (2002a).

4. In Europe long-term unemployment is considered to begin after twelve months; the figure corresponding to Argentina is six months.

5. In an example of the specific consequences of job insecurity, taken from a research project in which data on school-age adolescents are compared, researchers found that the school drop-out rate was greater

for young people from middle-class homes in which the parents' jobs were unstable than for those with a low but stable income level (Beccaria and Kessler 1999).

6. This is a way of asking for money in the street that carries a veiled threat of violence if the request is not met.

7. The most common modality is for a group of young people to block some public access, demanding money to let people pass.

CHAPTER 4

1. In this chapter the terms *ethnic marking* and *demarcation* will be used to refer to the processes and mechanisms that have marked with an ethnic identity the bodies of persons or groups and others that have demarked them in different situations.

2. In Argentina some members of patriotic institutions dedicated to watching over the image of the founding fathers consider the mention of such a possibility as an attempt to undermine historic veracity in general and the Argentine nation in particular. But across the river humble schoolteachers have always considered this as an example of the bonds uniting these frontier settlements with Argentina. Not only had San Martín been born there, but he, like they themselves, was the result of an encounter between Indians and Spaniards.

3. The indigenous population of Brazil was estimated to be between 236,000 and 300,000 in the 1990s, representing less than 0.2 percent of the total population (Ramos 1998, 3–4). In Argentina estimates run from 250,000 to 450,000, representing between 0.7 percent and 1.2 percent of the total population (Vázquez 2000, 133–34). The figures for both countries increased significantly in the most recent census; according to preliminary estimates, they have tripled. In Argentina, however, indigenous people play no part in the Argentine patriotic saga, whereas in Brazil they are considered "a powerful symbol of nationality" (Ramos 1998, 4).

4. A somewhat peculiar innovation is the growing role of Bolivians in the truck gardens on the outskirts of Buenos Aires. The demand for intensive labor is often supplied by a family or other network and, although precarious, truck gardening is also a means for progressing. Benencia (1997) postulated the existence of a "Bolivian ladder" whose rungs are laborer, middleman, renter, owner. Middlemen predominate

in a system in which Argentines provide the land and Bolivians provide the work. To progress, the family must have the capacity to save, which enhances the role of women as devisers of saving strategies.

5. Declarations by Guido Di Tella in London. Quoted in *Página 12*, June 11, 1995.

6. Ibid.

7. *Clarín*, June 17, 1995.

8. In ten months in 1994, around 23,638 arrests were made of immigrants from Peru, Uruguay, Chile, Bolivia, Paraguay, and Brazil. Federal police chief Adrián Pelacchi argued, "The immigratory aspect is one of the factors contributing to the lack of security in the city." According to declarations by Pelacchi himself, a total of 20,928 immigrants were forced to abandon the country for having committed "different violations," described as petty crime. For example, the violations include loitering, which permits the police to arrest someone waiting or walking around who "looks suspicious." Loitering is the subjective "crime" par excellence, being defined by dress or skin color rather than by an illegal act. This is why loitering was removed from the criminal code of the city of Buenos Aires in 1998.

9. *Clarín*, November 19, 1996. In 1995 the same poll—called Latin Barometer and carried out in a number of South American countries—measured the confidence felt regarding people with other nationalities: in last place once again were Chileans (34 percent) and Bolivians (36 percent) (*Página 12*, November 8, 1995).

10. In the case of native people, the paradox is "the recent appearance (two decades ago!) of indigenous peoples thought of by others and by themselves as the original inhabitants of their countries" (Pacheco de Oliveira 1999b, 11).

CHAPTER 5

1. The *piquete*, or picket, is the device used to keep strikebreakers from entering their place of employment during a strike. Present-day *piqueteros* or picketers are unemployed men and women who form a line across streets and highways that impedes the flow of traffic. The term had negative connotations when it first appeared in certain mass media organs. But the connotation became positive when *piquetero*

organizations picked up the term, using it to refer to themselves and in slogans like "*piqueteros carajo,*" or "picketers god damn it," during demonstrations.

2. It can be alleged that, despite common identities such as *piqueteros,* a high degree of fragmentation continues to exist. This is true, but it is also true that, unlike the phase analyzed by Schuster and Pereyra (2001) in which demands themselves were fragmented, now divisions correspond to splits within the political left and center-left in Argentina (see Svampa and Pereyra 2003).

3. Interview with Patricia Aguirre, a specialist in Nutritional Anthropology, *Clarín,* July 20, 2003.

4. The concept of nutritional security was stipulated as a human right by the FAO (UN Food and Agricultural organization) in 1974, on the basis of documents going back to 1924 that named it as one of the basic human rights; it figures as such in the organizational minutes founding the FAO, as well as in its preamble.

5. At the time the graph was drawn up, July 2002, data showed purchasing power was lower than in 1989.

6. Articles appeared in *El País* in Spain ("El trueque sustitye a la economía formal," January 27, 2002) and the newspaper *Liberation* in France (July 15 and August 22, 2002).

7. The Roundtable Dialogue, which included representatives from the Catholic Church, government officials, representatives from labor unions and of the unemployed, and members of the barter club, was organized as an ongoing intersectorial debate on ways to overcome the crisis.

8. A major Argentine mass-circulation newspaper.

9. The term arose out of the combination of two supposed pillars of the consumer society: production and consumption.

10. The recipient of a stipend collects a fixed amount of money monthly, currently set at 150 Argentine pesos (approximately $50) since 2002.

11. Andrea D'atri interviewed Celia Martínez; the interview can be read at http://www.andreadatri.com.ar/articulo13.htm

Bibliography

AA.VV. (1997a) *Mercosur: un atlas cultural, social y económico.* Buenos Aires: Instituto Herbert Levy y Manrique Zago Ediciones.

AA.VV. (1997b) *O mercosul e a integração Sul-Americana: Mais do que a economia. Encontro de culturas.* Brasília: FUNAG.

Acuña, C. (1995) *La nueva matriz política argentina.* Buenos Aires: Nueva Visión.

Acuña, C., and Smith, W. (1994) "The political economy of structural adjustment." In *Latin American political economy in the age of neoliberal reform,* ed. W. Smith, C. Acuña, and E. Gamarra. Miami: University of Miami Press.

Aguirre, P. (2004) *Pobres gordos, ricos flacos.* Buenos Aires: Capital Intelectual.

Alberdi, J.B. (1915) *Bases y puntos de partida para la organización política de la República Argentina,* Buenos Aires, La Facultad.

Altamirano, C. (ed.) (1999) *La Argentina en el siglo XX,* Buenos Aires, Ariel, 1999.

Altimir, O. (1979) *La dimensión de la pobreza en América Latina.* Santiago de Chile: CEPAL.

Altimir, O., and Beccaria, L. (1999) *Distribución del ingreso en la Argentina.* Santiago de Chile: CEPAL. Serie Reformas conómicas 40.

Armony, V., and Kessler, G. (2004a) "Imágenes de una sociedad in crisis. Cuestión social, pobreza y desempleo." In *Los veinte años de democracia,* ed. M. Novaro and V. Palermo. Buenos Aires: EDHASA.

Armony, V., and Kessler, G. (2004b) "La fin d'un pays de classe moyenne. Fragmentation, paupérisation et crise identitaire de la société argentine." *Problèmes d'Amérique Latine* 51:83–109.

Auyero, J. (2001a) *La Política de los Pobres. Las prácticas clientelistas del peronismo.* Buenos Aires: Manantial.

Auyero, J. (2001b) "Introducción." In *Parias Urbanos. Marginalidad en la ciudad a comienzos del milenio,* ed. L. Wacquant. Buenos Aires: Manantial.

Azpiazu, D. (2003) *Las privatizaciones en la Argentina. Diagnóstico y propuestas para una mayor equidad social.* Buenos Aires: Miño y Dávila-CIEPP-OSDE.

Azpiazu, D. (2005) Las privatizadas I & II. Ayer, hoy y mañana. Buenos Aires: Claves para todos.

Balán, J. (1990) "La economía doméstica y las diferencias entre los sexos en las migraciones internacionales: un estudio sobre el caso de los bolivianos en la Argentina." *Estudios Migratorios Latinoamericanos* 5: n. 15–16.

Balán, J. (1992) "The role of migration policies and social networks in the developments of migration system in the Southern Cone." In *International migrations systems. A global approach,* ed. M. Kritz, L. Lim, and H. Zlotnik. New York: Oxford.

Bayón, C., and Saraví, G. (2002) "Vulnerabilidad social en la Argentina de los años noventa: impactos de la crisis en el Gran Buenos Aires." In *Trabajo y ciudadanía. Los cambiantes rostros de la integración y exclusión social in cuatro áreas metropolitanas de América Latina,* coord. R. Katzman and G. Wormald. Montevideo: Universidad Católica del Uruguay/Pontificia Universidad Católica de Chile.

Basualdo, E. (2003) "Las reformas estructurales y el Plan de Convertibilidad durante la década de los noventa. El auge y la crisis de la valorización financiera", in *Realidad Económica* N° 200, IADE, Buenos Aires, November 16–December 31, 2003.

Beccaria, L. (1993) "Reestructuración, empleo y salarios en la Argentina." In *El desafío de la competitividad. La industria argentina in transformación,* ed. B. Kosacoff. Buenos Aires: Alianza Editorial, CEPAL.

Beccaria, L., and Kessler, G. (1999) "Heterogeneidad social y fuentes de desventajas: el caso argentino." Paper presented at III Reunión de la Red de Economía Social, Lima, 1999.

Beccaria, L., and Vinocur, P. (1991) "La pobreza del ajuste o el ajuste de la pobreza." Working paper no. 4, UNICEF Argentina.

Becker, H.S. (1963) *Outsiders: Studies in the sociology of deviance.* New York: Free Press.

Beltrán, M.E., and Reges, C. (2003) "Mujeres migrantes en la ciudad de Buenos Aires." In *Programa todas: "Buenos Aires. Ciudad con migrantes,"* dirección General de la Mujer: Gobierno de la Ciudad de Buenos Aires, 15–28.

Benencia, R., and Gazzotti, A. (1995) "Migración limítrofe y empleo: precisiones e interrogantes." Paper presented in las V Jornadas de Colectividades, Buenos Aires, IDES, mimeo.

Benencia, R. (1997) "De peones a patrones quinteros. Movilidad social de familias bolivianos en la periferia bonaerense," en *Estudios migratorios latinoamericanos*, n° 35, Buenos Aires, 63–102.

Benza, S. (2002) "El festejo patrio peruano en Buenos Aires: la ritualización del mundo migrante y multiplicidad de la peruanidad." In *Estudios migratorios latinoamericanos*. Buenos Aires: in press.

Boccia Paz, A. (1999) "'Operativo Cóndor': ¿un ancestro vergonzoso?" In *Cuadernos para el debate*, no. 7. Buenos Aires: IDES.

Botana, N., and Waldmann, P. (1988) *El impacto de la inflación*. Buenos Aires: Universidad Di Tella.

Briones, C. (1998) "(Meta) cultura del estado-nación y estado de la (meta) cultura." In *Série Antropologia*, no. 244. Departamento de Antropologia/UnB.

Canevaro, S. (2005) "El caso de los jóvenes peruanos y el ingreso a la Universidad de Buenos Aires," Seminario Internacional de Migraciones, Universidad de Costa Rica, San José.

Canitrot, A. (1979) La disciplina como objetivo de la política económica. Un ensayo sobre el programa económico del gobierno argentino desde 1976, Buenos Aires: CEDES.

Carvalho, J.M. de (1990) *A formação das almas: o imaginário da República do Brasil*. São Paulo: Companhia das Letras.

Casaravilla, D. (2003) "Crisis social, discurso y xenophobia." In *Programa todas: "Buenos Aires. Ciudad con migrantes,"* Dirección General de la Mujer: Gobierno de la Ciudad de Buenos Aires, 15–28.

Cavarozzi, M. (1999) "El modelo latinoamericano. Su crisis y la génesis de un espacio continental." In *América Latina: un espacio cultural en un mundo globalizado,* ed. M.A. Garretón. Bogotá: Andrés Bello.

Cefai, D. (1994) "Type, typicalité, typification. La perspective phénoménologique." In *L'enquete sur les catégories. Raison Partiques,* ed. B. Fradin, L. Queré, and J. Widner, 5. Paris: Editions de l'EHESS.

CEPAL (2003) Panorama Social de América Latina. Santiago de Chile: CEPAL.

Cerruti, M. and Grimson, A. (2005) "Buenos Aires, neoliberalismo y después,", en Portes, A.; Roberts, B.; Grimson, A.: *Ciudades latinoamericanas*, ed. A. Portes, Roberts, B., and Grimson, A. Buenos Aires, Prometeo.

Chiaramonte, J.C. (1997) *Ciudades, provincias, Estados: Orígenes de la Nación Argentina*. Buenos Aires: Ariel.

Chiricos, T.G. (1987) "Rates of crime and unemployment: An analysis of aggregate research evidence." *Social Problems* 34:187–212.

Cisneros, A. (2000) "Discurso" In *Argentina-Brasil a visão do outro*, AA.VV. Brasília: FUNAG.

Clementi, H. (1996) "Hacia una historiografía diferente." In *La dimensión cultural del Mercosur*, comp. H. Clementi. Buenos Aires: CEA-CBC-UBA.

Cortés, R., and Marshall, A. (1999) "Estrategia económica, instituciones y negociación política en la reforma social de los '90." *Desarrollo Económico* 39:154. Buenos Aires. pp. 195–212.

Cravino, M.C., Fournier, M., Neufeld, M.R., and Soldano, D. (2002) "Sociabilidad y micropolítica en un barrio *bajo planes*." In *Cuestión social y política social en el Gran Buenos Aires*, org. L. Andrenacci. Buenos Aires: UNGS-Ediciones al Margen.

Damill, M., Frenkel, R., and Maurizio, R. (2002) Argentina: Una década de Convertibilidad. Crecimiento, empleo y distribución del ingreso, Buenos Aires: CEDES.

Delamata, G. (2002) "De los 'estallidos' provinciales a la generalización de las protestas en Argentina. Prespectiva y contexto en la significación de las nuevas protestas." *Nueva Sociedad* 182 (November–December).

Escolar, D. (2000) "Identidades emergentes en la frontera argentino-chilena." In *Fronteras, naciones e identidades*, comp. A. Grimson. Buenos Aires: CICCUS-La Crujía.

Esping-Andersen, G. (1990) *The three worlds of welfare capitalism*. Princeton, N.J.: Princeton University Press.

Fajn, G. (ed.) (2003) *Fábricas y Empresas Recuperadas. Protesta social, Autogestión y rupturas en la Subjetividad*. Buenos Aires: Ediciones del Instituto Movilizador de Fondos Cooperativos.

Faur, E. and Gherardi, N. (2005) "Sexualidades y reproducción: La perspectiva de los derechos humanos." In Equipo Latinoamericano de Justicia y Género (ed.), *Informe sobre Género y derehcos humanos: vigencia y respeto de los derchos de las mujeres en la Argentina*. Buenos Aires: Biblos.

FIEL. (1988) *Regulación y estancamiento. El caso argentino*. Buenos Aires: Ediciones Manatial.

Filgueira, C. (2002) "Estructura de oportunidades, activos de los hogares y movilización de activos en Montevideo (1991–1998)." In *Trabajo y ciudadanía. Los cambiantes rostros de la integración y exclusión social en cuatro áreas metropolitanas de América Latina*, coord. R.Y. Katzman and G. Wormald. Montevideo: Universidad Católica del Uruguay/Pontificia Universidad Católica de Chile.

Freeman, R.B. (1983) "Crime and unemployment." In *Crime and public policy,* ed. J.Q. Wilson. San Francisco: ICS Press.

Frigerio, A. (1999) "Prefácio." In *Axé Mercosul. As religiões afro-brasileiras nos países do prata,* ed. A.P. Oro. Petrópolis: Vozes.

Frigerio, A. (2000a) "Blacks in Argentina: Contested representations of culture and ethnicity." Ponencia presentada en el Congreso de Latin American Studies Association, Miami, March.

Frigerio, A. (2000b) "Fronteras de papel: el pánico sobre el 'éxodo industrial a Brasil' en los medios de comunicación argentinos." *Revista de Investigaciones Folclóricas* 15. Buenos Aires.

Gayol, S., and Kessler, G. (2002) *Violencias, delitos y justicias en la Argentina.* Buenos Aires: UNGS-Manantial.

Gonzalez Bombal, I. (2002) "Los clubes del trueque." In *Sociedad y sociabilidad en la Argentina de los noventa.* Buenos Aires: UNGS-Biblos.

Gordillo, G. and Leguizamón, J.M. (2002) *El río y la frontera: aborígenes, obras públicas, y Mercosur en el Pilcomayo.* Buenos Aires, Biblos.

Gorelik, A. (1993) "Figuras urbanas." *Punto de Vista* 47 (December): 9–12.

Gorelik, A. (2000) "História Brasil. Argentina. Enfoques comparativos e paralelismos históricos. Comentarios." In *Argentina-Brasil a visão do outro,* AA.VV. Brasília: FUNAG.

Grimson, A. (1998) "El otro (lado del río). Periodismo de frontera y producción de significaciones sobre Nación y Mercosur en Posadas." In *Tesis de Maestría en Antropología Social.* UNaM: Posadas.

Grimson, A. (1999) *Relatos de la diferencia y la igualdad. Los bolivianos en Buenos Aires.* Buenos Aires: Eudeba.

Grimson, A. (2000a) "El puente que separó dos orillas." In *Fronteras, naciones e identidades,* comp. A. Grimson. Buenos Aires: CICCUS-La Crujía.

Grimson, A. (2000b) "Cortar puentes, cortar pollos. Conflictos económicos y agencias políticas en Uruguayana (Brasil)–Libres (Argentina)." *Revista de Investigaciones Folclóricas* 15. Buenos Aires.

Grimson, A. (2003a) "La nación después del deconstructivismo." *Sociedad* 20–21. Buenos Aires.

Grimson, A. (2003b) "La vida organizacional en zonas populares de Buenos Aires." The Center for Migration and Development, Working Series Paper, Princeton University, CMD Working Paper *03-15-e. Publicado in Internet: http://cmd.princeton.edu/papers/wp0315e.pdf.

Grimson, A. (2003c): *La nación en sus límites*, Barcelona, Gedisa.

Guber, R. (1997) "Reflexiones sobre algunos usos nacionales de la Nación." *Causas y Azares* 5 (autumn): 59–66. Buenos Aires.

Guber, R., and Visacovsky, S. (1998) "De las 'antropologías nacionales' a la nacionalidad en la antropología. Un caso argentino." Brasília, Série Antropologia, 235, Departamento de Antropologia/UnB.

Halperin Donghi, T. (1995) *Proyecto y construcción de una nación (1846–1880)*. Buenos Aires: Ariel.

Halpern, G. (1999) *Migración paraguaya en Buenos Aires y procesos políticos*. Tesis de licenciatura en Ciencias de la Comunicación, Facultad de Ciencias Sociales (UBA).

Heymann, D. (2000) *Políticas de reforma y comportamiento macroeconómico: la Argentina en los noventa*. Buenos Aires: CEPAL. Serie Reformas Económicas no. 61.

Heyman, D. and Kosacoff, B. (ed.) (2000) *Desempeño económico en un contexto de reformas, Tomo 1*, CEPAL EUDEBA, Buenos Aires.

Hintze, S. (1989) *Estrategias alimentarias de sobrevivencia*. Buenos Aires: Centro Editor de América Latina.

Hintze, S., ed. (2003) *Trueque y economía solidaria*. Buenos Aires: UNDP-UNGS-Prometeo.

Hirsch, S. (2000a) "Misión, región y nación entre los guaraníes de Argentina." In *Fronteras, naciones e identidades*, comp. A. Grimson. Buenos Aires: CICCUS-La Crujía.

Hirsch, S. (2000b) "Tirando el mal del otro lado de la frontera: brujería e identidad cultural entre los guaraníes de Bolivia y Argentina." *Revista de Investigaciones Folclóricas* 15. Buenos Aires.

Hirschman, A. (1970). *Exit, voice and loyalty. Cambridge*, Mass: Harvard University Press.

Hoffman, K., and Centeno, M.A. (2003) "The lopsided continent: Inequality in Latin America." *Annual Review of Sociology* 29:363–90.

Instituto Nacional de Estadísticas y Censos. (1996) *La población no nativa de la Argentina, 1869–1991*. Buenos Aires: INDEC.

Instituto Nacional de Estadísticas y Censos. (1999) Inmigración y empleo, Buenos Aires, INDEC.

Instituto Nacional de Estadísticas y Censos. (2003) *Informe de Coyuntura*. Buenos Aires: INDEC.

James, D. (1990), *Resistencia e integración. El peronismo y la clase trabajadora argentina. 1946–1976*, Buenos Aires: Sudamericana.

Jelín, E. (1998) *Pan y Afectos. La transformación de las familias.* Buenos Aires: Fondo de Cultura Económica.

Jelín, E., and Feijóo, M.C. (1980) *Trabajo y familia en el ciclo de vida femenino: el caso de los sectores populares en Buenos Aires.* Buenos Aires: CEDES.

Karasik, G. (2000) "Tras la genealogía del diablo. Discusiones sobre la nación y el estado en la frontera argentino-boliviana." In *Fronteras, naciones e identidades,* comp. A. Grimson. Buenos Aires: CICCUS-La Crujía.

Kaztman, R. (2003) "Seducidos y abandonados: el aislamiento social de los pobres urbanos." Montevideo: IPES Working Paper 1.

Kaztman, R., Beccaria, L., Filgueira, C.H., Golbert, L., and Kessler, G. (1999) *Vulnerabilidad, activos y exclusión social en Argentina y Uruguay.* Santiago de Chile: O.I.T.-Fundación Ford.

Kessler, G. (1998) "Le processus de paupérisation de la classe moyenne argentine." PhD in sociology, Ecole des Hautes Etudes en Sciences Sociales, Paris.

Kessler, G. (1999) "L'experience de paupérisation de la classe moyenne argentine." *Culture and Conflicts* 35:35–74.

Kessler, G. (2002a) *Pobreza, vulnerabilidad y riesgo en la comunidad judía uruguaya.* Montevideo: American Jewish Joint-Ediciones Banda Oriental.

Kessler, G. (2002b) "Entre fronteras desvanecidas. Lógicas de articulación de actividades legales e ilegales en los jóvenes." In *Violencias, delitos y justicias in la Argentina,* ed. S. Gayol and G. Kessler. Buenos Aires: Manantial.

Kessler, G. (2004) *Sociología del delito amateur.* Buenos Aires: Paidós.

Kessler, G. and Espinoza, V. (2003) *Movilidad social y trayectorias ocupacionales en Argentina: ruptura y algunas paradojas del capital de Buenos Aires.* Santiago de Chile: CEPAL. Serie Políticas Sociales.

Kusznir, J.C. (1997) "En busca de la seguridad pérdida." *Novedades Económicas* (April): 38–52.

Larrañaga, O. (1999) *Distribución de ingresos y crecimiento económico en Chile.* Santiago de Chile: CEPAL. Serie Reformas Económicas no. 35.

Lavaca (2005): Sin Patrón. Fábricas y empresas recuperadas por sus trabajadores. Una historia, una guía. Buenos Aires: Lavaca Editora.

Leite, D. (1994) "Universidade e Integração: A Centralidade do Conhecimento", en Morosini, Marília Costa (org.): *Universidade No Mercosul,* San Pablo, Cortez Editora.

Lomnitz, L. (1975) *Cómo sobreviven los marginados*. México: Siglo XXI.

Lomnitz, L., and Melnick, A. (1991) *Chile's middle class: A struggle for survival in the face of neoliberalism*. Boulder, CO: LACC Studies on Latin America and the Caribbean.

Lo Vuolo, R., Barbeito, A., Pautassi, L., and Rodriguez, C. (1999) *La pobreza... de la política contra la pobreza*. Buenos Aires. Miño y Dávila-CIEPP.

Lozano, C. (1994) *Estructura actual de la clase trabajadora*. Buenos Aires: IDEP, Cuaderno 29.

Luzzi, M. (2005) *"Refaire le marché?* Paris: L'Harmattan.

Mantucelli, D. and Svampa, M. (1997) La plaza vacía. Las transformaciones del Peronismo. Buenos Aires: Losada.

Mármora, L. (1994) "¿De qué son culpables los inmigrantes?" *Clarín*, Buenos Aires, 15 de diciembre.

Mármora, L. (1999) "Mitos xenófobos." *Tres puntos*, no. 84, febrero.

Marshall, A. 1994. *Estabilidad y cambio en la estructura de salarios*. Paper presentaed at II Congreso Nacional de Estudio del Trabajo, Buenos Aires, 22-26 august.

Merklen, D. (1991) *Asentamientos en la Matanza. La terquedad de lo nuestro*. Buenos Aires: Catálogos.

Mesa-Lago, C. (1999) "Desarrollo social, reforma del Estado y de la seguridad social, al umbral del siglo XXI." *Reforma y Democracia*, no. 15, Caracas, October.

Minujin, A. (ed.) (1992) Cuesta Abajo. *Los nuevos pobres: efectos de la crisis en la sociedad argentina*, Buenos Aires: UNICEF/Losada.

Minujin, A., and Kessler, G. (1995) *La nueva pobreza en Argentina*. Buenos Aires: ed. Planeta

Murillo, V. (2004) Sindicalismo, coalicion partidaria y reformas de mercado. Madrid: Siglo XXI.

Navarro, I. (1997) "En Argentina el crimen paga." *Novedades Económicas* (April): 17–28.

Navarro, M.F. (1995) "Democracia y reformas estructurales: explicaciones de la tolerancia popular al ajuste económico." *Desarrollo Económico* 35 (139): 443–66.

Neiburg, F. (1997) *Os intelectuais e a invenção do peronismo*. Buenos Aires, San Pablo: Universidade de São Paulo.

Nun, J. (2001) "El enigma argentino", en *Punto de Vista*, n° 71, December 2001.

Nun, J. (2001) Marginalidad y exclusión social. Buenos Aires: Fondo de Cultura Económica.

Offe, C. (1987) "Democracy against the welfare state." *Political Theory* 15 (4).

Oteiza, E., and Aruj, R. (1995) "Inmigración real, inmigración imaginaria y discriminación en la Argentina." Paper presented in las V Jornadas de Colectividades, Buenos Aires, IDES, mimeo.

Oteiza, E., Novick, S., and Aruj, R. (1997) *Inmigración y discriminación. Políticas y discursos.* Buenos Aires: Universitaria.

Pacheco de Oliveira, J. (1999a) "Apresentação." In *A viagem da volta. Etnicidade, política e reelaboração cultural no Nordeste indígena*, org. J. Pacheco de Oliveira, 7–10. Río de Janeiro: Contra Capa.

Pacheco de Oliveira, J. (1999b) "Uma etnologia dos 'indios misturados'?" In *A viagem da volta. Etnicidade, política e reelaboração cultural no Nordeste indígena*, org. J. Pacheco de Oliveira, 11–40. Río de Janeiro: Contra Capa.

Palomino, H. (2003) "El movimiento de trabajadores de empresas recuperadas", In Revista *Sociedad*, 20/21, Facultad de Ciencias Sociales, Universidad de Buenos Aires.

Pereyra, B. (2001) "El lugar de las organizaciones civiles de extranjeros residentes in Buenos Aires." Buenos Aires, marzo, inédito.

Pompei, E. (1999) "Las consecuencias sociales de la distribución," *Enoikos* (abril): 69–79.

Portes, A., and Hoffman, K. (2003) *Las estructuras de clase en América Latina: composición y cambios durante la época neoliberal.* Santiago de Chile: Serie Políticas Sociales no. 68.

Portes, A., and Walton, J. (1976) "The politics of urban poverty." In *Urban Latin America.* Austin: University of Texas Press.

Prelorán, M. (1995) *Aguantando la caída.* Buenos Aires: Ediciones Mutantia.

Programa Nacional de Asistencia Técnica para la Administración de los Servicios sociales en la República Argentina (PRONATASS). (1991) *La diferenciación interna de los asalariados del Gran Buenos Aires.* Buenos Aires: PRONATASS-Ministerio de Trabajo y Seguridad Social.

Przeworski, A. (1991) *Democracy and the market.* New York: Cambridge University Press.

Ramos, A. (1998) *Indigenism: Ethnic politics in Brazil.* Madison: University of Wisconsin Press.

Ratier, H. (1971) *El cabecita negra.* Buenos Aires: CEAL.

Rebón J. (2004): Desobedeciendo al desempleo. La experiencia de las empresas recuperadas. Buenos Aires: Ediciones Picaso/La Rosa Blindada.

Recondo, G., comp. (1997) *Mercosur. La dimensión cultural de la integración.* Buenos Aires: CICCUS.

Repetto, F. (2001) *Gestión pública y desarrollo social en los noventa. Las trayectorias de Argentina y Chile.* Buenos Aires: Universidad de San Andrés-Prometeo.

Rofman, A. (1997) *Convertibilidad y desocupación en la Argentina de los '90: análisis de una relación inseparable.* Buenos Aires: CEUR-CEA-UBA.

Rofman, A., and Romero, L.A. (1973) *Sistema socioeconómico y estructura social en la Argentina.* Buenos Aires: Amorrortu.

Romero, L.A. (1994) *Breve Historia Contemporánea de la Argentina.* Buenos Aires: Fondo de Cultura Económica.

Rosanvallon, P. (1995) *La nouvelle question sociale.* Paris: Seuil.

Rouquié, A. (1981) *Poder militar y sociedad política en la Argentina.* Buenos Aires: Emecé, Tomo I.

Sábato, H. (2000) "Comentarios." In *Argentina-Brasil a visão do outro,* AA.VV. Brasília: FUNAG.

Sarmiento, D.F. (1977) *Facundo,* Caracas, Biblioteca Ayacucho.

Schvarzer, J. (1983) Martínez de Hoz: la lógica política de la política económica. Buenos Aires: CISEA.

Schuster, F., and Pereyra, S. (2001) "La protesta social en la Argentina Democrática. Balance y perspectivas de una forma de acción política." In *La protesta social en la Argentina: transformaciones económicas y crisis social en el interior del país,* comp. Giarraca. Buenos Aires: Alianza.

Schutz, A. (1987) *Le chercheur et le quotidien.* Paris: Méridiens Klincksieck.

Segato, R. (1998) "Alteridades históricas/Identidades políticas: una crítica a las certezas del pluralismo global." In *Anuário Antropológico/97.* Río de Janeiro and Brasília: Tempo Brasileiro.

Semán, P. (2000) "El pentecostalismo y la religiosidad de los sectores populares." In Sennet, R. (1998) *The Corrosion of Character. The Personnal Consequences of Work in the New Capitalism.* New York: Norton & Company.

Desde abajo. La transformación de las identidades sociales, ed. M. Svampa. Buenos Aires: Biblos.

Sigal, S., and Kessler, G. (1997) "Comportements et représentations dans une conjoncture de dislocation des régulations sociales. L'hyperinflation en l'Argentine." *Culture et Conflits* 24–25: 35–72.

Sinisi, L. (1998) " 'Todavía están bajando del cerro.' Consideraciones estigmatizantes de la alteridad en la cotidianidad escolar." Paper presented in las VI Jornadas sobre Colectividades, Buenos Aires, IDES, October.

Stolcke, V. (1999) "New rhetorics of exclusion in Europe." *International Social Science Journal,* 51 (159): 25–35.

Svampa, M. (2002) *Los que ganaron. La vida en los countries y barrios privados.* Buenos Aires: Biblos.

Svampa, M. (2005) *La sociedad excluyente.* Buenos Aires: Taurus.

Svampa, M., and Pereyra, S. (2003) *Entre la ruta y el barrio. La experiencia de las organizaciones piqueteras.* Buenos Aires: Biblos.

Torrado, S. (1994) Estructura social de la Argentina: 1945-1983. Buenos Aires: Ediciones de la Flor.

Torrado, S. (2003) Historia de la familia en la Argentina moderna (1870–2000). Buenos Aires: Ediciones de la Flor.

Touraine, A. 1991. " Face à l'exclusion." *Esprit,* 169: 7–13.

Torre, J.C. (1998) El proceso político de las reformas económicas en América Latina. Buenos Aires: Paidós.

Trpin, V. (2004). Aprender a ser chilenos. Identidad, trabajo y residencia de migrantes en el Alto Valle de Río Negro. Buenos Aires: Antropofagia.

Ugalde, P., and Prieto, J.J. (2001) *Caracterización de la clase media en Chile durante los noventa.* Informe Preliminar. Santiago de Chile: Facultad de Ciencias Sociales. Universidad de Chile.

Vázquez, H. (2000) *Procesos identitarios y esclusión sociocultural. La cuestión indígena en la Argentina.* Buenos Aires: Biblos.

Vega Ruiz, M.L. (2001) *La reforma laboral en América Latina.* Lima: OIT.

Vidal, H. (2000) "La frontera después del ajuste." In *Fronteras, naciones e identidades,* comp. A. Grimson. Buenos Aires: CICCUS-La Crujía.

Wilson, T. (2000) "Nación, estado y Europa en la frontera de Irlanda del Norte", en Grimson, A. (comp.): *Fronteras, naciones e identidades,* Buenos Aires, CICCUS-La Crujía, 2000: 121–138.

Williams, R. (1980) *Marxismo y literatura*. Barcelona: Península.

Williams, R. (1983) *Keywords*. New York: Oxford University Press.

Williams, R. (1996) "La tecnología y la sociedad." *Causas y Azares*, no. 4. Buenos Aires.

Wormald, G., Cereceda, L., and Ugalde, P. (2002) "Estructura de oportunidades y vulnerabilidad social: los grupos pobres en la Región Metropolitana de Santiago de Chile en los años 90." In *Trabajo y ciudadanía. Los cambiantes rostros de la integración y exclusión social in cuatro áreas metropolitanas de América Latina*, coord. R. Katzman and G. Wormald. Montevideo: Universidad Católica del Uruguay/ Pontificia Universidad Católica de Chile.

Newspapers Cited

Clarín

La Nacion

Paginaiz

Index

X

Y